How to
Understand
the Man you
Love

How to Understand the Man you Love

RICK JOHNSON

SPIRE

© 2012 by Rick Johnson

Published by Revell
a division of Baker Publishing Group
PO Box 6287, Grand Rapids, MI 49516-6287
www.revellbooks.com

Spire edition published 2020
ISBN 978-0-8007-3825-9

Previously published in 2012 under the title *The Marriage of Your Dreams* and in 2015 under the title *Understanding the Man You Love*

Printed in the United States of America

Unless otherwise indicated, Scripture quotations are from the Holy Bible, New International Version®. NIV®. Copyright © 1973, 1978, 1984, 2011 by Biblica, Inc.™ Used by permission of Zondervan. All rights reserved worldwide. www.zondervan.com. The "NIV" and "New International Version" are trademarks registered in the United States Patent and Trademark Office by Biblica, Inc.™

Scripture quotations labeled NKJV are from the New King James Version®. Copyright © 1982 by Thomas Nelson. Used by permission. All rights reserved.

20 21 22 23 24 25 26   7 6 5 4 3 2 1

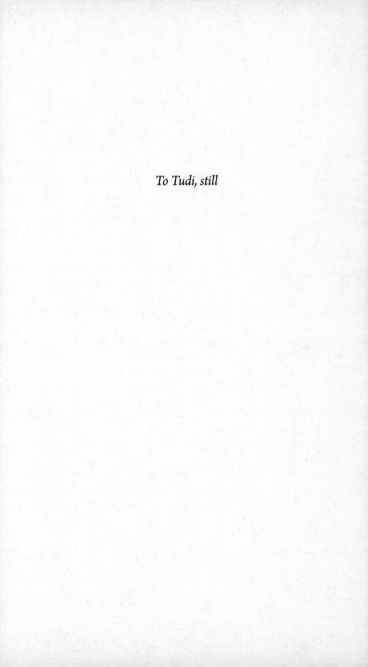

To Tudi, still

Contents

After he disconnected from Adrian, he sat there trying to figure out why Kate was still mad at him. She'd been mad when he first told her he was going to be gone for a month and wouldn't tell her why, and he understood that, but then she came to his house, and she didn't seem so mad at all, and then for some reason she got mad all over again, and now she was refusing to talk to him, and he couldn't keep up with how her moods kept changing.

The easiest way to understand it, he guessed, was to not bother trying, to recognize the obvious fact that women were different from men, and to keep in mind that he, Stonewall Jackson Calhoun, did not understand them, and he just had to accept it. Women didn't think like men, they didn't have the same emotions as men, they didn't behave like men. They didn't love the way men did, either.

Calhoun loved women—or at least, he loved Kate Balaban—but he had no idea what made her tick. In fact, he was in awe of her. She was utterly unpredictable, and as far as he was concerned, that made her endlessly fascinating.

Now she'd decided not to talk to him, and there was no sense in trying to figure out why, because the reason was buried somewhere in that inscrutable woman-ness that he loved about her but that sometimes frustrated him beyond tolerance.

Excerpt from William G. Tapply, Dark Tiger

The Woman of His Dreams

The idea for this book stemmed from several women asking for a book similar to my book on authentic masculinity, *The Power of a Man*. They wanted to know how to be the best wife possible and how to best meet the needs of their husbands (many of whom were unable or unwilling to articulate their needs and desires to their wives). They wanted to know what men really need and want from a wife so they can fulfill those expectations. They said most books only address the physical aspects of a woman that are attractive to a man. They felt they could not live up to that "Barbie" factor and so were discouraged. Instead of guessing, they wanted to understand a "standard" that men have of women. They wanted to know (from a man) *all* the things that are attractive in a woman and what a man needs or expects from a wife. After all, if you don't know what is expected of you how are you supposed to meet those expectations? I think many women feel like they are playing a losing game in this arena.

As usual when I write books for women, I asked a large number of females for their input. I was curious about what *they* wanted to know most about men. I surveyed a wide range of women, both young and mature, married and single. I talked to women from as many races, religions, and backgrounds as I could. These women were surprisingly (even shockingly) open about the questions they had regarding men (you'll see some of their questions with my answers at the end of each chapter). I also surveyed a number of men— particularly about their relationships with their mothers, which seems to be a topic most women are interested in.

I received quite a number of responses from women who feel the way this woman does:

> This particular topic—although probably needed—does not appeal to me and in fact seems demeaning to women. If the church weren't so busy telling wives that "they need to please their man" maybe the men would need to stop being so spoiled and blaming their wives for their own poor communication skills and simplistic approach to life.

Hmmm, I wonder what she really thinks? But I believe she has a valid point, at least in some regard.

I also received just as many responses from women at the other end of the spectrum who feel like this woman:

> I really wish women could just get over themselves. The world doesn't revolve around us, and maybe instead of unloading all of our blah-blah-blah on our husbands, who aren't equipped to handle that sort of mass "woman-for-mation," we should meditate and learn how to quiet our minds and save our need to "emotionally vomit" for our

girlfriends. Then we'd be more apt to put on something sexy and meet our man at the door at the end of the day than to unload on him and then freak out that he doesn't understand what's going on.

I'm not sure that those radically diverse answers were specifically helpful, but they did confirm to me how complicated women are regarding most issues, including this one.

I know some of you are thinking, "Not another book on what men need! I spend my whole day meeting the needs of other people. What about my needs? When is someone going to write a book about what I need?" Believe me I sympathize with you. I realize the brunt of nourishing families and maintaining relationships falls upon women. I also know that men in general tend to be a bit self-focused or even selfish. I acknowledge that this is a heavy burden and that without women there would be no civilization (in fact, no human race at all). But women have been uniquely qualified and gifted to be able to meet these challenges. Part of what makes this responsibility easier is understanding your motivations and the expectations of those whose lives you fulfill and complete.

Many women's frustrations stem from wondering, "What does he expect from me? I'm doing everything the best I can. Doesn't he know I'm at the end of my rope here?" Maybe if, instead of guessing, you are able to put your efforts into more efficient and productive endeavors, it will help ease that burden.

Women seem to be driven to make all things in their lives— relationships, marriages, children—better. Part of the challenge most women face is they interpret their husband's needs through their own filter. This book gives women an open and honest look inside the world of a man's needs (which even he might not recognize) and helps them understand how best to use their powerful influence to have a satisfying and exciting relationship.

My previous book, *The Man Whisperer*, focused exclusively on how a woman can *communicate* with her husband. This book addresses a wider range of topics about how a woman can satisfy and support the needs of her man. It will help a woman understand a man's sexual needs and how he feels about work. It will help her encourage his emotional growth, recognize common traps most men fall into, encourage him as a father (and in his other roles in life), and know what men admire and desire most in their wives. This book gives women a look at the insides of a man to understand how he thinks, how he operates, and what motivates him. It also sets a standard of desirable femininity from a man's perspective.

Hopefully, it will help a wife become the woman of her man's dreams—the woman her man fantasizes about.

one

What's with His Mother Anyway?

> To a mother, a son is never a fully grown man; and a son is
> never a fully grown man until he understands and accepts
> this about his mother.
>
> —*Unknown*

While researching this book, I discovered something that caught me completely by surprise. A number of women asked if I would be willing to explore the role that a man's relationship with his mother plays in the relationship he develops with his wife. They reported feeling like they're paying for the perceived sins of their husband's mother, both in positive and negative ways. One woman said it this way:

> I find myself curious about the thoughts men have about their mothers and how those thoughts are manifested in the women they choose to surround themselves with. I believe you have explored the edges of this theme, at least

in your talks, but I'm wondering what men actually have to say about their moms and mothering. I find that they seem to have very strong emotions about mothers and mothering but I'm always feeling baffled about the thought processes behind those emotions. Maybe they really just don't *think about it at all*, but they act on those emotions.

For some reason (despite having written several books on the mother-son relationship) the thought had never occurred to me to investigate the importance a man's mother plays in his marriage relationship.

A man's relationship with his mother is a complicated thing. His mother too often makes him feel like a little boy. She may still treat him (even if unknowingly) like the boy he was. Even if she doesn't, she still evokes memories (perhaps unconsciously) of a time when he was helpless, powerless, and dependent upon a woman. She likely changed his poopy diapers, breast-fed him, and wiped his snotty nose when he cried like a baby. The very instinct he has to break away from his mother in order to achieve manhood necessitates that he distance himself from her emotionally because of the danger she has to lure him back into boyhood. Through no fault of her own she represents what he struggled so hard to leave behind—boyhood and the alluring comfort and safety of being taken care of by a woman.

And yet clearly, if a boy is to become a man he must at some point break away from those tightly wrapped arms of motherhood. He must break away from the world of women and step into the world of men—the band of brothers, if you will. Boys who do not make this transition are stuck wandering through a sort of purgatory, never comfortable in either world. This breaking away process can be painful for mom, and often necessitates that a boy, at least temporarily, distance himself from his mother.

If you've read *That's My Son* or *That's My Teenage Son* you know that mothers are vitally important in the fundamental development of sons and in helping to create healthy masculinity. Fairly or unfairly, mothers seem to be at the core of a lot of people's (both men and women) issues, getting blamed for insecurities, guilt, and every other mental health problem imaginable. Every mother with sons I know is well aware of this stereotype and is worried about "screwing him up." The caricature of the patient on the psychiatrist's couch blaming his mother for his mental problems is standard fare in today's culture. However, the moms who aren't concerned about it may be the very ones who should be worried the most. And women too have plenty of blame they hold against their own mothers—everything from driving them crazy to laying guilt trips on them for not being married and producing grandchildren.

With that in mind, let's unwrap some of the ways a man's mother influences his life, including the choices and decisions he makes regarding women.

Cutting the Apron Strings

> Breaking free from the delicious security of mother love can be a painful rupture for either mother or son. Some boys can't do it. Some mothers can't let it happen because they know the boy is not ready to leave her; others are simply not ready to give up their sons.
>
> —*Frank Pittman,* Man Enough

Since my relationship with my own mother was the only experience I had to go by (and that's not exactly a stalwart example), I sent out a questionnaire to approximately fifty men from various backgrounds asking about specific areas of their relationship with their mother. I was somewhat pessimistic about how many men would respond, as the topic is a touchy one and men don't generally respond well to requests for personal information anyway. Imagine my astonishment when almost every man answered the questionnaire! I was also surprised by the open and honest answers they gave to my questions. It was almost as if they had been waiting for an opportunity to explore and express this part of their lives. So, what did I learn from this survey?

The question that comes up time and again is, "Do men marry their mothers?" The answer is—sort of. A mother's influence and importance in his early life coupled with his association with his father's model during adolescence might either consciously or unconsciously steer a man to choose a woman similar to the one his father did. Or conversely, a negative experience might encourage him to seek just the opposite kind of woman than his mother. In healthy situations, a boy's mother probably does provide a model of love, nurturing, and respect that he would want to reproduce in his marriage. In hindsight my wife is very similar to my mother in many ways, except she has healthy virtues in place of some of my mother's more unhealthy qualities. Did I recognize this when I married her? No, and it would have probably been a little creepy if I had. Most men I queried did not recognize that similarity until they were presented with my question, and upon reflection realized that there were in fact many areas in which their wives paralleled their mothers' personality traits.

Those who did not see similarities generally tended to have intentionally married a woman with the opposite character traits than their mothers—frequently because of a traumatic childhood relationship with her.

Most men don't like to talk about their mothers—they certainly don't like to talk badly about her or hear anyone else do so. They tend to either love and respect her (sometimes to a fault), or want to ignore her to keep her from bothering them. No man *wants* to hurt his mother, so they often stay away from her as much as possible rather than risk hurting her feelings. As they become independent, many men quickly become irritated by her habits, uncomfortable with her proximity, and view her as uninteresting or even exasperating—possibly as an unconscious consequence of breaking those childhood bonds. Her loving actions now seem like meddling, fussing, and worrying—reminiscent of boyhood. In these circumstances, a man can barely tolerate more than a day or two in his mother's company. Men quickly learn to make only perfunctory visits or brief obligatory phone calls to their mothers.

Those men with healthy, loving relationships with their mothers seem rather few and far between. Realistically, after he becomes a man, a son has little "need" for his mother in his life except for nostalgic purposes. While a mother is indispensible to a boy while he is still a child—providing loving, caring, and nurturing support and compassion—after he grows up a man does not (and should not) expect that kind of adoring affection from his mother. After he marries, his wife takes over many of the loving and nurturing duties that a mother fulfills early in life. This is unlike his relationship with his father, whom he may need even more than at any time in his life.

Freud's theory of the Oedipus complex is a governing metaphor for masculine development, and the adult man who maintains a close relationship with his mother runs the risk of being stigmatized as a "mama's boy." Some social scientists now challenge that theory, asserting that men do not have to psychologically separate themselves from their mothers in order to become masculine. They posit that this need to separate is limited to Caucasian culture and is not shared in African-American or Asian culture, where men do not have a conflict between manhood and a close loving relationship with their mothers.[1] Additionally, men from other cultures, such as Italian or other Mediterranean backgrounds, seem to have closer relationships with their mothers than is typical in the US. And mothers in other cultures typically have great power over their sons and their relationships. Many men in Middle Eastern, Indian, and Jewish cultures have (or at least appear to have) a lifelong close relationship with their mothers.

Role Model

A man's mother models several important roles in his life. She is the first role model of femininity, and she is the first role model of female sexuality. She models how a woman relates to and treats a man, and she models how a woman should expect to be treated by a man. She is the model of how a woman respects and loves a man and how a woman receives love from a man. Mothers are often the barometer of a man's perception of how much respect a woman deserves from a man.

Nearly all the men I questioned reported they were consciously aware of the way their mothers treated their fathers. This often determined (again, consciously or unconsciously) the way they expected to be treated by their wives—and often influenced the way they themselves treat their wives. One man expressed it like this: "My parents were codependent. She covered up his abusive behavior. Everything was always fine, fine, fine. We don't talk about our problems. I married a woman who knew how to play the same game. Since my mom kowtowed to my father, I expected the same treatment. I learned to control her with smoldering anger, just as my dad controlled my mother."

Men who grow up in chaotic homes learn to survive. They bring that survival strategy into their marriages. They will subconsciously try to create the same kind of chaos so they can use their survival strategies. This is why counseling and recovery is so important—so this kind of game playing becomes unnecessary.

Even when mom treats dad with too much respect, it can cause problems later on, as evidenced by this man's memories:

> Mom treated dad with reverence. He could do little wrong most of the time. She always made sure I understood the sacrifices he was making for the family, since he spoke little of that; he was quite the modest man and still is. They would argue at times, sometimes loudly and ferociously, but they ensured that we kids saw them work it out. During those arguments she never emasculated him as far as I remember. Yes, it absolutely has influenced how I expect my wife to treat me. That has been an area of some contention as I have, sometimes mistakenly, pointed that out to my wife in the heat of the moment.

Not only that, but a boy's mother has a huge influence on how a boy sees himself as a man. Mothers can short-circuit the fragile connection between boyhood and manhood with their words and attitudes. A mother's influence on how a boy feels about himself as a man is very significant. A mother who despises men can make life difficult for a boy. Especially for women who have been hurt by men in their life this can present a real challenge. Paul Coughlin says it this way: "Give him a mother who was beaten by her father. She'll do the best she can to attack burgeoning manhood in her boys. She'll look at powerful men with contempt and then use her verbal acumen to castrate young male souls. Thereby she condemns a boy's manhood: When she criticizes his father, the boy will struggle with the belief that he's the fruit of defective seed."[2]

On the other hand, mothers who respect and admire healthy masculinity can make a boy believe he was created for greatness. Through her affirming power she can lift him up to be and do things he could never become or accomplish without her powerful influence in his life. Either way a man's mother plays a huge influence in his life and on his masculinity.

A woman who has attended several of my seminars says this about what she learned regarding her influence as a woman: "I found that your talks very much inspired me to take a hard look at the woman I presented my boys day in and day out. Do I look groomed and ready for my day each morning? Do I speak intelligently and kindly or am I screeching? Am I allowing the men around me to be men or am I trying to control them? These are the kinds of thoughts and reflections I've come away with."

Most men shudder and will not even address the issue of the influence of their mother's sexuality. There is no doubt, however, that a mother's healthy or unhealthy sexuality influences her son significantly. Mothers are the first and most important role model of female sexuality. A woman who has been wounded and has not healed in this area can pass those unhealthy attitudes on to her sons (and daughters).

The Influence of Women on Masculinity

Women play a significant role in developing masculinity. Women influence the *type* of men a culture creates in several ways. One way is through the men they choose to have sex with. Men conform to the requirements and rules to which they are held accountable. This applies to the area of relationships just as much as to the business or sports world. Whether good or bad, the percentage of women having multiple sexual partners has greatly increased in recent decades, even among Christians. Bottom line, the character of the men a woman sleeps with encourages that character in all men. If enough women have sex with men of low character, that is what all men will aspire to be like. If they only sleep with men of noble character, then that is the standard all men will strive to live up to. In the same way, if all women required men to marry them before engaging in sexual intercourse, that is the standard men would live up to.

Either way, their offspring (male and female) will tend to follow in those footsteps. If mothers sleep with men who abuse and abandon them, their daughters will likely be attracted to men of similar character. The role model fathers set for boys is very important in how they live life. A father who is absent or abandons his offspring is much more likely to produce a son who follows in his footsteps. Women who choose to procreate with men who abandon them leave a legacy of abandonment for their sons to follow. Likewise, a father who abuses his wife passes that legacy on to his son. The modeled behavior of both the mother and father influences future behavior in children of both genders. Not always—of course there are examples of people who are nothing like their parents. But more often than not we seem to be programmed to unconsciously mimic those behaviors and make choices that lead us to end up in the role that was modeled for us.

The other way women influence masculinity in a culture is by how they choose to raise their sons. If women raise sons without a healthy male influence in their lives (either by choice or consequence) it negatively impacts a boy's life for as long as he lives. A mother can influence a boy's character by the environment she raises him in. By allowing and encouraging healthy male influences, allowing him to learn by trial and error, not rescuing him to the extreme, and instilling character values in him by holding him accountable—while still nurturing him—she creates a whole man who will face the world confidently. This kind of man will lead his family and contribute to the betterment of society.

She's Driving Me Crazy

I've spoken to a lot of men who had negative relationships with their mothers. And even those who have average or good relationships seem to be concerned about a number of traits their mothers exhibit.

Many men reported feeling like their mothers continue to fuss over them even into manhood. They felt like she was always asking personal questions, worrying about them, and generally butting into their business. One man said this about his wife's tendency to be "over-involved" in their sons' lives: "My adult sons have learned to just not answer any of their mother's questions. They've learned that if they answer one question it leads to dozens more. I try to tell her to leave them alone, but she cannot seem to stop from pestering them—it is not in her nature."

Many men also reported that their mothers continued to give them unsolicited advice even after they became a man. They frequently felt like they were being lectured. One man said, "Of course my mom gives me unsolicited advice—she's a mother!"

Giving unsolicited advice to a boy is necessary, but to a man it is unwanted at best and insulting at worst. It says to a man that he is not competent enough to solve his own problems. Moms of course give advice because they love and care about their children (no matter how old they are) and are just trying to be helpful. Many men told me they made a conscious decision to tune out or ignore their mothers rather than getting angry when she started giving advice they neither wanted nor needed.

One thing that I *know* drives men crazy is when their wives do not treat them as if they are fully adult. It reminds them of their mothers. Women sometimes have a tendency to treat their husbands as if they are children. Sometimes men will buy into that mentality and actually start acting like children, while others rebel, becoming frustrated and insulted. For instance, I've heard at least one wife ask her husband, "Did you wash your hands? How long ago did you wash them?" That would make me want to respond with something along the lines of, "Maybe" or "Yesterday." Women get so wrapped up in running the household they don't realize those are questions you ask the kids, not a grown man. I don't think they even know they are being critical or insulting; it's just another item on the checklist for running a smooth home.

A man's mother can have an adverse effect on him by the things she says (or said) to him. For instance, her scorn, contempt, and negative criticism can easily gore a boy's self-esteem. Not only that, but she influences his personality. One man said it this way: "My mother was an alcoholic. Her 'hero-worship' of poor examples of masculinity—like men who got into fistfights behind the bar—formed my personality in ways that I would never have anticipated and in hindsight did not want. I was programmed to emulate these examples of manhood that she admired in an unconscious attempt to get her affection and approval. As an adult I transferred that unhealthy behavior of constantly seeking my mother's approval onto my wife."

Another way that mothers can harm their sons is by encouraging too much loyalty from them. For instance, boys who have been put in the position of trying to protect their mothers from an abusive husband or boyfriend can develop overprotective feelings toward their mothers. The unfortunate outcome of this situation is that a boy cannot protect her from a man, and so he will invariably end up feeling inadequate and ineffectual. A boy in these circumstances can enter into a sort of emotional incest where he becomes fixated on his mother. This is detrimental in his other relationships. Most women know to run from a man who has too close a relationship with his mother—it's unhealthy. And yet, women are also leery (rightfully so) of a man who disregards or disrespects his mother.

Unhealthy mothers also have the ability to cause their sons pain and anguish. Here's what another man said about his mother:

> She has the ability to hurt me deeply. She can also make me feel incredibly guilty even when I'm right. Those are both emotions that males prefer to keep at arm's length as much as possible. Frankly, it is frightening to deal with her because she has all the cards in her hand—she knows my vulnerabilities better than anyone and I cannot fight back because I have been programmed that a man must love and respect his mother. Even the ultimate, last resort defense that a man has—the ability to defend himself physically— is null and void because you can't hit a woman, especially your mother. Despite the propensity that she has to injure me deeply, I am still instinctively programmed to desire her love, respect, and pride.

Some mothers are clingers who never let their sons go. They don't understand or care that when a man marries a woman, he cleaves to her and breaks away from the bond with his mother and father. His wife is now his main priority and the most important female in his life, not his mother. These moms use undue influence, either through guilt or manipulation, to maintain a stronghold over their sons. She inserts herself into his life in unhealthy ways, making sure that he considers her opinions, feelings, and needs above those of his wife and children. Such a woman is hard to break away from, as she has usually made some significant sacrifice in her own life for her son, thus using guilt and gratitude as levers to pry her way into his life. These women often view their sons as surrogate husbands.

Mothers who were wounded or abused in childhood and never recovered can pass along that damage to their offspring. These women often have addictive personalities (drugs, alcohol, shopping, sex, food, etc.) and/or might have some form of mental illness (bipolar disorder, anxiety disorders, psychosis, or personality disorders such as obsessive-compulsive or paranoia). Such moms frequently lash out in their pain as a way of numbing it (the old adage "misery loves company" comes to mind). They do not love themselves and so are incapable of loving others. They cause great destruction to themselves and to their children.

And finally, other mothers use guilt and shame as leverage to get their own needs met through their children. One man said it like this:

> I've always had a basically good relationship with my mom. She was really the leader in our home, as my dad has always been affable but passive. There were times in my later years at home when she probably over-shared with me about her and Dad's relationship problems, but I felt privileged to be trusted with the information. Now I look back and see that interaction as a little emotionally incestuous. I grew up as an approval-seeking perfectionist, largely because neither of my parents expressed themselves emotionally, withholding affection and praise. My mother did and does try to change people by using disapproval as one of her primary tools. I grew up with that, and it still snags me sometimes.

You and His Mother

It's probably only natural that there is at least some amount of tension or friction between a wife and her mother-in-law. Most mothers are pretty protective and even somewhat possessive of their sons (like fathers are with their daughters). She might (even though unconsciously) resent another woman usurping her role as *the* woman in his life as well as being replaced in his affections. After all, for years he was her little baby boy—he was the male child she heaped her love, hopes, and dreams upon. Many moms spoil their sons in ways they would never think of or tolerate with their daughters. And frequently mothers feel that no woman is ever good enough for their son.

Many men (although not all) I questioned admitted that at least initially (early on) their mothers did meddle in their marriage to one degree or another. But the majority believed that their mothers did not do it maliciously but more as a sense of duty ("That's what mothers do, right?").

Most mistakes come when a man will not clearly cut the apron strings with his mother and thus allows animosity to develop and exist between the two most important women in his life. A man should make it clear that his wife is the most important priority in his life. Not that he shouldn't still love and respect his mother, but he should cleave to his wife, placing her needs first. Again, the goal is not to dishonor or disrespect his mother, just to place his priorities in the proper perspective. Unfortunately—possibly because he wants to avoid conflict or even feels intimidated by his mother—too many men allow this issue to fester and harm their marriage relationship. One man described his experience this way: "In my case, the two had some really tough times getting along. That, at some point, forced my hand and I had to really work to cut the proverbial umbilical cord and cleave to my wife."

Many men I spoke with were anxious about confronting any tension between their wives and mothers. Again, emotional situations are uncomfortable or even frightening for most men, and they tend to avoid them whenever possible. Here's one man's description of how he dealt with his wife and mother not getting along:

> Very carefully! I was falling into trying to defend my mom all the time and it communicated to my wife that my loyalties had not transferred over. At a certain point, I had to mature enough to recognize that I needed to stand up to my parents and communicate certain expectations I had in terms of the respect they needed to demonstrate toward my wife. Once I did that, the tensions seemed to dissipate, but it was years before we got to that point and required creating some distance between our home and my parents.

The following example seems to accurately illustrate many situations I heard about. Bob's wife felt her mother-in-law was frequently being critical of her. Bob had learned to ignore his mother when she started giving unsolicited advice (rather than confronting the issue in a messy emotional conflict) and couldn't understand why his wife didn't just do the same. Of course, his wife felt that Bob was not defending her and was hurt and angry by his seeming ambivalence and lack of gallantry. As the situation continued to escalate, all parties got more frustrated and bitter—much to Bob's growing dismay. As the vitriol between his wife and mother deepened he became more intimidated and unwilling to open this "Pandora's Box" of emotional conflict. After all, emotions (especially raw emotions) are uncontrollable and frightening to most males. Without firm leadership and decisiveness by Bob, this situation will eventually explode in one direction or another with tragic consequences. Either his mother will get hurt because Bob breaks off all relations with her to appease his wife, or he will allow the animosity to continue festering and eroding his relationship with his wife.

I'll admit that I don't have any special insight into the psychological complexities of the female psyche. But women often seem to have some sort of unspoken emotional or psychological competition that goes on between them. I don't pretend to understand this undeclared battle, but it is there and is often very confusing to most men.

A wise (and healthy) mother realizes that a wife supplanting her role as the most important woman in her son's life is the natural course of life, and she allows her son to go without clinging to that "queen bee" status she has held in his life since birth. A mother who won't willingly relinquish this role frequently resorts to emotional manipulation to control him. She attempts to subtly undermine or sabotage his relationship—all very innocently of course.

Like most men, your husband probably desires his mother's approval. The admiration, respect, and pride of the important women in his life (wife, mother, sisters, etc.) are fundamental to a man being satisfied and content with his life.

His Mother-in-Law

> Mother-in-law: a woman who destroys her son-in-law's peace of mind by giving him a piece of hers.
>
> —*Author Unknown*

There doesn't seem to be a lot of middle ground regarding a man's relationship with his mother-in-law. The common stereotype is that the mother-in-law is a meddler who despises her son-in-law and undermines his marriage relationship at every turn. Understandably, the son-in-law is not thrilled with that attitude and responds by hating her and begrudging his wife spending time with her mother. This illustration is sort of the stereotypical "husband/mother-in-law who can't stand each other" relationship modeled in older TV programs like *The Flintstones*.

The other side is that many men have genuinely close relationships with their mother-in-law. She is often an ally or confidante that he can rely upon to help smooth the stormy waters of marital conflict. Especially if he did not have a mother or had a strained relationship with his mother, his wife's mother can be a blessing.

Ladies, let me say this: your mother is probably important to you, but your husband is more important. If there is friction between your mom and your husband, you have an obligation to ensure that she shows him the proper respect that he deserves as your man. It is a wife's duty to protect and defend her husband's honor in areas where he cannot. Your mother's attitude toward him is one of those areas. If it's fair for a wife to expect her husband to intervene when his mom doesn't respect her, then it's just as appropriate for a husband to expect his wife to do the same with her mom.

~~~

Real Questions from Real Women

Q: Do most men find themselves re-creating the family environments they grew up in?

A: Not intentionally as a rule. They may unconsciously re-create their home life, but many say they purposefully reject it if they came from a bad home situation. Those few who had a very happy home life growing up may try to intentionally reproduce that environment.

Q: How do men make peace with their mothers and the "mother" they find in their wives?

A: Mostly they ignore the issue.

Q: Is there a time in a man's life that lends itself to redefining his relationship with his mom? Is this related to God ordering men to "cleave unto their wives"?

A: Many men never address this issue until it is too late, either when their mother passes away or when their marriage relationship is wounded too deeply. As men get older, they soften and often yearn to have a closer relationship with their mothers.

Q: What do men think and say about this?

A: Most men say the issue is too complex and messy to feel comfortable sorting through. Additionally, they do not want to hurt their mothers.

Q: **What are some things mothers have done that have empowered good men? What do men say?**

A: Mothers who hold boys to firm boundaries and intentionally do not rescue them too often do their boys a great favor by allowing them to fail and learn from their mistakes. Failing and persevering until they succeed creates positive self-esteem and self-image in boys and teaches them many important life lessons.

Q: **How does a man think about his relationship with his mother and his treatment of her, and how does he think about his wife and his treatment of her?**

A: Men who respect their mothers are probably likely to respect their wives. Conversely, men who disrespect their mothers are frequently disrespectful to their wives. Maybe not to all women, but probably to those they are in intimate relationships with.

two

His Father

His Role Model

Every father should remember that one day his son will follow his example instead of his advice.

—*Unknown*

Sam was always afraid of his stepfather's arrogant violence and seeming invincibility. The violence and anger he grew up with was a source of chaos, fear, and frustration. Because of his stepfather's contempt toward him, Sam was compelled to overachieve to try and prove that he was worthy of respect. As he grew, he did everything he could to protect himself: he wrestled and boxed throughout high school, and became adept at hand-to-hand combat after joining the military.

During the middle of his first tour of duty, Sam got a phone call from his sister. His stepfather had beaten his mother again—this time bad enough that she had to be hospitalized. Sam immediately requested leave to go home and put a stop to this behavior once and for all. When he arrived and confronted his stepfather, he was stunned at how frightened the man was. Here was this huge bully who had physically wounded, psychologically taunted, and emotionally humiliated him throughout childhood, now cowering in fear. He could see the fear in his eyes. He could smell it radiating off him in waves. Sam was disgusted. But he was also secretly afraid—afraid because he wondered if he was a coward too by virtue of having been raised by one. Sam's greatest fear was that he would become like his stepfather.

Sam has carried this fear throughout his life, and it affected his relationships with his wife and children.

A Man's Most Important Influence

In order to best understand a man, it is important to look at the most important factors that made him who he is. A man's father (or his male role models as a child) may be the biggest influence he has in life. A man is heavily influenced not only by his father's genes but by his father's (or father figure's) behavior in a variety of ways. The legacy left for him and the model that was displayed for him growing up contributes to determining his path through life. Some men intentionally reject this model, while others consciously or unconsciously mimic what was modeled for them—either good or bad. Men with good father figures tend to walk in the footsteps modeled for them, more easily leading positive and productive lives.

Conversely, many men who claimed they would never leave their wife and children frequently find themselves in those same circumstances. Often a man leaves when he is the exact same age that his father was when he left, or he leaves when his sons are the same age he was when his father left—identical to the model his father set for him. These men usually don't recognize how they ended up in that situation and are quite surprised when I point out those similarities.

Others, sometimes even against their will, follow in the footsteps of addictions, infidelity, or abuse that were modeled for them by their father figures. We seem to have an almost unconscious propensity or preprogramming, or possibly even a genetic predisposition, to stumble along and make decisions that put us in the same situations modeled by our core caregivers. Because males are such visual learners, we internalize and later emulate what we observed in the important men in our lives.

One of the greatest men of my lifetime (in my opinion) was Coach John Wooden. In his book on Coach Wooden's life philosophy, author Pat Williams says this about him and the role of his father: "I have been searching for the wellsprings of this man's greatness as a leader and a human being. I've become convinced that both the greatness and the goodness of John Wooden can be traced to his father."[1]

One way to understand your husband is to understand the relationship he had or has with his father and how that affects the man he is today. That knowledge can give you some insight into why he acts the way he does, why he thinks what he does, and even what he might do in future situations. For women who have not had the opportunity to know their father-in-law, ask your husband what his life was like as a boy.

Consider entering into this discussion when you are walking in the woods together or in some other relaxing situation. Gently and slowly direct the conversation to what his father was like and their relationship as he was growing up. Most men are somewhat reluctant to talk about this issue but are very forthcoming once you are able to get them talking.

Father Knows Best

No matter how old he is, a man needs a relationship with his father (or at least a father figure). The curse for so many men is that they never had that relationship. A man needs a father to bless him and help propel him into the world. He needs him to teach him, model masculine roles for him, and encourage him as he struggles through life. Even as grown men we all yearn for that kind of approval and blessing from our fathers. Fathers provide wisdom from their own experiences, knowledge about relationships, and information on how the world works. They act as coaches, teachers, and trainers for their sons or those they mentor.

All males need older males to guide them through life. It is the natural order of things. Young boys look up to older boys for guidance on how to act. Older boys look up to young men, and young men look to their older counterparts. In fact, at all stages of life we need mentors. Young fathers need older fathers to help with questions and problems. *What did you do when your kids did this? How do I handle the pressures and responsibilities of leading a family? Did you go through these challenges in your marriage?* Even older males whose children are grown and gone look up to others. Now that my kids are out of the house, I need a retired man to tell me and show me how to approach the next stage of my life. I need an older man who has traversed that path to tell me things like, *What will life look like? What kind of challenges will my marriage face? What can I expect as my body ages, and what health issues will arise?*

Often we don't even realize we are looking for guidance from an older male. If we have good role models, then we naturally tend to make good decisions and choices. With poor role models, however, we tend to make unhealthy or even destructive choices. The advice we get and the examples set for us are what we tend to emulate.

For a man who had an absent or abusive or just neglectful father, this model will impact his journey throughout life. For men with those types of fathers it is imperative that they find a way to reconcile with and forgive their fathers any grievances (real or imagined) in order to grow and heal from those wounds. These grievances keep males from becoming the kind of men, husbands, and fathers that they are capable of and that they want to be. They are roadblocks that prevent growth for a man in all his roles.

Further complications arise in this scenario because fathering in particular is a learned skill, one that men aren't typically born with. Without a positive role model early in life, it's extremely difficult for a boy to learn how to be a man, father, husband, or even how to love his wife.

Boys who grow up without healthy men in their lives face serious disadvantages later on. They have to discover on their own how to become a man—a huge and frightening task. Boys who grow up fatherless often end up confused, scared, and dangerous. Not only do they fail to understand their role as provider and protector of their families, they also are afraid to pursue a life of significance. Boys who don't receive this kind of training are confused as to their roles in life, never finding security or satisfaction.

And such is the dilemma that many boys and young men face today—the prospect of growing up never really knowing what it means to be a man or understanding their role as a husband and father.

Daddy Doesn't Live Here Anymore

What we remember from childhood we remember forever—
permanent ghosts, stamped, inked, imprinted, eternally seen.

—*Cynthia Ozick*

What happens to males and their masculinity without proper training? How and why do certain "generational cycles" get passed from one generation to the next?

God has given men, especially fathers, tremendous power to influence the lives of those around them. In particular, the lives of women and children are hugely impacted by what a man does or doesn't do with his life. Men who are good fathers and husbands mightily bless the lives of their wives and children. Men who are absent, abusive, or unconnected have just as big of a negative influence in the lives of their families. For a boy, his father is *the* most important role model in his life.

Children are often "preprogrammed" to exhibit certain tendencies or make specific choices merely by what was modeled for them when they were growing up. Traumatic events during childhood are especially engrained in a child's psyche. Old programming, like old habits, dies hard.

When fathers abuse or abandon sons, their sons repeat those same behaviors—not always, but pretty often. Even though they might not want to, they almost cannot help imitating what was modeled for them.

The effects of being raised without a father are huge hurdles for men to overcome. Author and psychologist Michael Gurian says this about young men today:

> Boys under 25 in this country are approaching masculine meltdown. Because of a lack of male role models in their lives, they have no idea what a man is, how a man acts, how he feels, or what he lives for. They have no vision of what men do. And many of them are angry. Fatherless children are crippled children. In their rage against their fatherless "wounds" they often commit acts of violence. Boys without an older male involved in their lives have no accountability. They tend to drift into themselves, into a world of fantasy and isolation.[2]

Many men have been wounded by fathers who themselves were damaged or by having had no positive male role model to learn under. We then stagger and stumble through life searching for roles and behaviors that fit comfortably enough to survive, all the while yearning for we know not what.

Author John Sowers describes it this way: "The fatherless boy lives with the nagging accusation that he will never be adequate, never measure up, never really be a man. For the young man who lives in shame, manhood seems just out of reach."[3]

I have spoken with numerous directors of homeless shelters and domestic abuse shelters, and every one of them tells me that, upon reflection, fathers are at the root of all their clients' problems. One woman told me, "I've worked in this industry for thirty-six years. Now that I think about it, every single one of my clients had either no father or an abusive father."

Boys who have never had healthy masculinity modeled for them face an extremely difficult, if not impossible, task—becoming a good man. Since healthy masculinity is rarely modeled in the movies, on television, or in our cultural heroes, they will never understand how to think, act, and behave like a man without the presence and guidance of a real man in their lives.

Effects of Fatherlessness on Boys (and Men)

Over the years our ministry has been involved in several opportunities to mentor fatherless boys. These experiences have given me a firsthand look at some of the significant challenges facing boys raised without fathers.

One of the challenges we see in fatherless boys is their lack of physicality. Many fatherless boys spend large amounts of unsupervised time in front of the television or video games, which is unhealthy on so many levels. These boys also do not learn how to "do" things, which is what contributes to a male's self-image. When boys do not learn how to do things or fix things, they feel inadequate. Little things that we might take for granted—such as how to drive a nail, catch a baseball, dribble a basketball, ride a bike, use a pocketknife safely, hike in the woods, build a campfire—are all the things that boys without dads do not learn and therefore feel inadequate because of. Learning how to do things gives boys a healthy sense of self-esteem and confidence in life.

Older boys often need to be taught skills such as shaving and other appropriate personal hygiene. You'd be surprised at the simplest things you or I take for granted that fatherless boys do not know how to do. And because it is embarrassing to ask, they often stumble through life without learning.

I recently met a young man from this type of background. He did not know how to properly shake a man's hand, look him in the eye, and greet him properly. Additionally, he was disheveled in appearance and had very bad breath, which was compounded by invading my personal space while talking to me. The thought occurred to me that boys and young men without proper training in these simple areas of life are at a huge disadvantage. The first step to getting any job is knowing how to shake someone's hand and engage in some amount of appropriate interpersonal communication. Another requirement in building any kind of a relationship is basic personal hygiene and social protocol. Without those skills, young men will not be able to function, much less succeed, at even the simplest level in life. Not being able to obtain a job, maintain healthy friendships, or find a girlfriend creates hopelessness, erodes self-esteem, and ostracizes them from healthy male role models. All this then leads to anger. Anger then leads to destructive behavior.

These young men also frequently do not learn important character traits such as self-discipline, perseverance (not quitting), honesty, courage, and respect for women (mother) and others. Many of these boys do not learn these character traits, not because their mother doesn't value them, but because they are more readily learned and accepted coming from an older male. This again places them at a big disadvantage in life.

Another issue we observe in fatherless boys and men is the unwillingness to accept challenges. Because they have no confidence and a natural reluctance to experience humiliation through their failures, many of these boys (or men) do not receive the valuable lessons and self-esteem garnered from failing and persevering until they succeed. Without a man to push them beyond their self-imposed limits, they seldom learn the value of or gain the self-esteem from overcoming difficult odds and finally succeeding. They also become frustrated and quit the first time something becomes difficult. They tend to cry easier than most boys (as men they become angry easier). When they fall down and scrape a knee they will instantly cry and wait for mom (or another woman) to come and rescue them. However, if a man picks them up and dusts them off they recognize they are not really hurt and stop crying right away. Again, a male's presence helps to guide and encourage them to persevere until they succeed, thereby gaining the positive self-image and confidence to accept risk and attempt challenges in other areas of life. When these boys become men they are afraid to accept challenges for fear of failing. They also tend to quit faster when things become difficult.

Another observation we make in fatherless boys is the tendency they have to be somewhat "different." This isn't meant to be disparaging of these boys, but many (if not most) seem to have some sort of disadvantage. This disadvantage might consist of behavioral problems, speech impediments, emotional struggles, or even learning disabilities (frequently ADHD); but they generally have some sort of physical or emotional "issue" that sets them apart from their peers.

Approximately 9.5 percent, or 5.4 million children from ages four to seventeen, have been diagnosed with ADHD as of 2007. Boys (13.2 percent) are significantly more likely than girls (5.6 percent) to have ever been diagnosed with ADHD.[4] Children from fatherless homes are twice as likely to struggle with hyperactivity, conduct, and emotional disorders and have a social impairment.[5] They are also nearly four times more likely to experience major depression in adulthood, four times more likely to experience bipolar disorders, and nearly four times more likely to experience schizophrenia.[6]

Interestingly, the significant increase in diagnosis of ADHD, especially in boys, over the past several decades has perhaps coincidentally coincided with the increase in fatherless homes and the increase in a sedentary lifestyle that many boys lead. Without the opportunity for healthy outdoor activities, many boys lack an outlet to release their frenetic energy levels, which then manifest themselves in other distracting behaviors.

Perhaps too the lack of confidence (or anger) that manifests itself in a boy without older male role models magnifies any insecurities or perceived imperfections. Or perhaps the natural male coping mechanisms in fatherless boys are not modeled, and so they do not learn to appropriately deal with stressful situations and this then intensifies their behavior in unfamiliar circumstances. Often these differences cause them to be isolated and more comfortable in female company, which tends to be more compassionate and accepting. They tend to have trouble fitting in with their peer group.

Because they lack male role models, they have adapted to being around only women. This makes them uncomfortable around males. This also makes them loners or easier prey to fall in with any social group that does accept them, such as gangs of other fatherless boys or unhealthy male role models of all types.

Very often these males have been feminized (not effeminate) by having only female influences in their lives. They develop traits more associated with a feminine perspective such as passivity, indecisiveness, and an aversion to risk-taking. Carl Jung said that when a son is introduced primarily by the mother to feelings, he will learn the female attitude toward masculinity and take a female view of his own father and of his own masculinity. These boys only get to observe a feminine outlook on how to respond to life. They come to expect to be "rescued" by mom (or another female) and frequently will not try new things. In fairness to them, they don't know any better—mom has always rescued them. Perhaps because she feels guilty about his life circumstances she makes his decisions for him, solves his problems for him, and helps whenever possible to make his life easier. As these boys become older they become indecisive, passive, docile, and unable to commit to a relationship. They tend to rely on females to make all the decisions that govern their lives and seldom take on natural leadership roles. Boys who have been rescued their entire lives do not learn how to overcome obstacles. Whenever anything gets too difficult (such as marriage or raising a family) they quit. Quitting becomes a habit.

In addition, boys raised mainly under the supervision of women—mom at home, female teachers, female Sunday school teachers, female Cub Scout leaders—often experience insecurity over their identity as men. How can we expect boys, raised in close proximity to only women, to learn anything other than female responses to life situations?

These feminized men resist making decisions or taking action when they don't *feel* like doing something. They base their decisions on feelings and not principles. A feminized man needs group approval before committing. These men are afraid of making decisions and shun risks. They become dependent on women to take care of them, to make all the decisions for them. That's how they've been raised. This aversion to risk-taking keeps them from displaying leadership qualities and keeps them from pursuing their dreams and a life of significance.

One of the unfortunate traits of a feminized man is that when he looks for a mate, he marries someone like Mom—usually a strong woman who will make decisions and take care of him. Of course, his wife thinks this is great—at first. She's marrying a sensitive man with feelings after all. But she soon becomes frustrated at having to make all the decisions. The more she pushes him, the more passive he becomes. The more passive and indecisive he becomes, the more frustrated she gets, eventually losing all respect for him.

Often these boys and men are also angry—understandably so. Sometimes their anger is externalized and apparent in social or educational venues, and other times it is internalized into passive-aggressive behavior. They do not have a father to teach, protect, and empathize with their struggles. Frequently though, this anger is used to cover other emotions such as fear, humiliation, anxiety, vulnerability, or even pain. When boys do not have role models to teach them how to succeed in life, the world is a frightening place. And because it feels "unmanly" to be afraid, many boys and men then cover that emotion with one that feels more manly—anger. Unless these boys are taught to recognize this, they are doomed to believe they can solve any problem in life using anger and other unhealthy coping mechanisms. As these angry boys become adults they turn into angry men.

Because they were raised with a feminized vision of life, they tend to rely on females to make all the decisions that govern their lives and seldom take on natural leadership roles. As adults, the presence of other males in a man's life can help to guide and encourage him to look at the world with a masculine vision, to persevere through struggles until he succeeds, thereby gaining the positive self-image and confidence to accept risk and attempt challenges in other areas of life.

Fatherless boys and men are often uncomfortable in the company of other men. Our men's ministry group frequently takes fatherless boys along with us camping or on other father-son activities. Some of these boys are quite tender-hearted and loveable, but invariably are very immature. They have been mommy's little boy. These boys spend too much time in the company of women and become uneasy or uncomfortable in the company of men. Because they spend so much time around female authority figures they have developed feminized traits in their behavior. They do not understand the "rules" of masculine company. For instance, they talk too much, frequently interrupting men who are talking, and react emotionally inappropriately. They chatter incessantly without ever coming to a point in the conversation. These boys have not learned the unwritten "laws" of respect which men live by with one another. By interrupting the conversation with inappropriate anecdotes they quickly alienate other males who can become scornful and contemptuous of them, eventually shunning and ignoring them.

They are also often disrespectful because they have been allowed to act that way around the women in their lives. It requires men to reprimand them—often harshly—in order to teach them how to behave appropriately in the company of men. Otherwise, men and other boys will not want to be around them, further isolating them, with devastating consequences as they get older. If they do not learn these skills and "toughen" out of their "softness," they suffer throughout their lives. They do not understand the more rough-hewn behavior of men, especially in the outdoors. They need to learn not to fret over a cut; to ignore scrapes, bruises, and mosquito bites; and to be enthusiastic in the face of adverse conditions or disappointments (there is nothing worse than a whiny, gloomy, complaining companion on a camping trip). Around their mothers these boys have learned that all they have to do is complain or act petulant and mom or grandmother will go to great lengths to fix their problems. To become healthy, happy men, these boys need to learn to fix problems for themselves and not depend on women for their emotional well-being.

Not all males raised without fathers exhibit these traits. In fact, many men raised by their mothers turn out to be well-adjusted, good men. But more often I see young men exhibiting some or all of these behaviors. If your husband was raised without strong, positive male role models in his life, he may need to find some good men to hang around with, men who care about him and can teach him things he needs and wants to know. Finding and integrating into a group of men like that can be frightening for a man who is uncomfortable around other men—especially if he has never been accepted into the company of men before. But this is essential if he is to become greater than the experiences of his childhood. Masculinity bestows masculinity—he needs other men to pull (or push) him into manhood.

Legacy

When I was twelve years old, during one of my parents' drunken late-night arguments, I found out that my stepfather was not my "real" father. It was a devastating blow. Our relationship until then had seemed tense and a little strained, but not necessarily abnormal. However, from that point forward it seemed as if a dam had broken, and he mocked and criticized me until I grew to a size that made those actions imprudent. This caused a loss of self-assurance in me, which prompted me to try to overachieve to subconsciously prove to him that I was worthy. It also made me feel inadequate in front of him.

Until we understand how our upbringing affects us today, we cannot be the kind of father, husband, or man that we want to be or that God created us to be. To do otherwise allows that legacy to get passed down to our children.

The only way we can truly overcome the legacy that was set for us and break those generational cycles is to forgive our earthly fathers. The Bible clearly tells us to honor our mothers and fathers. But what if you were raised by a mother or father who acted (or acts) in ways that make it difficult to honor them? What are some practical ways in which a man can follow God's commandment and receive the blessing attached to it? Anyone raised by severely broken parents recognizes the frustration, difficulty, and sometimes *impossibility* of fulfilling that commandment.

Perhaps the best way to honor our parents under those circumstances is to live a life that would honor them. For example, through education, hard work, and the grace of God I was able to break the generational cycles of abuse, addiction, and divorce that were modeled for me. I have tried to live a life that would cause anyone looking on to say to my parents, "You must be so honored that your son is choosing to live a life that is dedicated to helping others." At that point I don't think it matters whether your parents recognize or appreciate the fact that you're living an honorable life. I believe that fulfills God's command to honor your mother and father.

Forgiveness and understanding are the biggest ingredients in the recipe for healing. Obviously, my relationship with the stepfather who raised me was never very good. I always thought I learned how to be the kind of father I didn't want to be from him, instead of the one I wanted to be. But when I look back on the kind of father he had, I think maybe he did the best he could with a limited amount of skills and knowledge. While there were many things he and my mother did that I would choose to be different in my childhood, I've come to believe that there was no malicious intent in his fathering (or my mother's parenting), merely ignorance tinged with apathy, pain, and possibly a pinch of panic. They were both wounded souls who had inadvertently passed on the legacy they received to the next generation. Their alcoholism was a coping mechanism to cover the wounds from childhood they were unable or unwilling to heal.

I don't think any man *wants* to be a bad father. I doubt if any man ever said to himself, "Okay, I've got a son now. I'm going to be the most terrible father I can possibly be, just to make his life miserable." Perhaps a very few men who have been hurt deeply by their fathers feel that way. But on the whole, I think every man would like to be a good father. We are hobbled by whatever role model we may have had. Until we heal (usually through God's grace and a lot of hard work), it is virtually impossible to break those generational cycles or sins.

Placing myself in my stepfather's shoes when he was a boy helped me to recognize the role model he had as a father. Once I saw him as a peer, as another man who struggled with sin and incompetence, it made it easier to let go of some of the grievances I held against him. If we accept the fact that our role models growing up play a big part in what kind of fathers we are, then understanding *why* our fathers parented the way they did is imperative to our own growth as fathers and as men. Every man I know has caught himself doing or saying something his father or mother did that he swore he would never, ever do. If a man struggles with forgiveness, I encourage him to try to see his father for what he was—not malicious but perhaps misguided, not evil but wounded and unforgiven.

And if your husband has never heard his father say the words "I love you," he needs to hear them. Otherwise, he will likely grieve for the rest of his life. We all have an inherent need to hear words of affection from our fathers. They are a blessing that propels us forward in life. I remember how good it felt when I truly believed that God loved me. I finally had a dad who loved me—it was such a relief.

The legacy that a man leaves behind is shaped by his heritage and specifically by his relationship with his father. At the very least, if he tries all that he can do to resolve whatever issues are between him and his father and still fails, he won't have regrets later in life. He will also have done his best to fulfill God's commandment to honor his father, and I believe God will honor that faithfulness.

Ladies, if your husband has unreconciled issues with his father I want to encourage you to help him. Men struggle with emotions and the intricacies of relationships anyway, but attempting to mend the powerful bond between a father and son is even more formidable, especially when broken and rusted over a long period of disuse. He needs your support and encouragement to muster the courage to tackle this challenge. He might be discouraged or even wounded deeply all over again. Attempting reconciliation takes great courage on his part and merits your admiration. This healing process can take a long time; it's rarely a one-shot deal. Your support will be the difference between success and failure. In fact, he may only attempt it because he realizes it is in the best interests of you and your children. Use all the power that God has given you as a helpmate, nurturer, and completer to stand with him and help him accomplish the journey. It will be worth all the effort and pain and hard work as he grows and becomes the kind of man, husband, and father that God created him to be.

REAL QUESTIONS FROM REAL WOMEN

Q: My husband has a lot of pain from growing up with an abusive father. He is angry all the time and is acting similar to his father. Is there anything I can do?

A: First of all, encourage your husband to seek professional counseling. It probably won't be easy to convince him to do this. Also, encourage him to find a small group of men he can meet with regularly. Often a men's Bible study group is helpful. The challenge for men in secular environments is that there are few if any groups like this available where men can meet with other men and get healing in a safe, comfortable environment. In my experience, it is difficult if not impossible to break those generational legacies that are passed down to us without God's intervention. Your husband needs to seek God's healing and forgiveness. Ultimately what your husband will need to do is reconcile and forgive his father before true healing can occur. This will likely be a long, slow, and arduous process that will need your constant support and compassion in order to be achieved. But trust me, it will be well worth it in the long run.

Q: Since his father left his mother and all the kids when they were at young ages, does this affect his

relationships and how he gets along with my kids and his own kids?

A: Absolutely! Men tend to imitate the behavior that was modeled for them by important masculine role models while growing up. Men who are able to break those patterns are "cycle-breakers" and should be commended highly.

three

His Relationships

His Most Difficult Challenge

> In Sicily, women are more dangerous than shotguns.
>
> —*Fabrizio,* The Godfather

The area that men struggle with the most in their lives is their relationships. Especially if they lacked good role models while growing up, men struggle with understanding what their role is in marriage, as a parent, or even as a friend. Because relationships are difficult (and often messy), men tend to shy away from them, preferring to isolate themselves or never engage fully in those associations they do have. Here's one reason why.

I recently watched a TV show on hippos on one of the nature channels. The show reminded me of the fact that in nature (and for most of humankind's history) the physically dominant male earned the right to mate with all (or at least the most desirable) of the females in the herd or group. This ensured that the strongest bloodlines would be put forth with the greatest chance for survival.

In early humans, physical strength and the ability to protect from predators (both human and animal) and provide food drew the healthiest, most willing, and most attractive number of females to mate with. This ensured the best possible scenario for survival of the family unit (healthy women and children). For thousands of years men learned to behave in ways that represented the ability to fulfill the roles of protecting and providing in order to mate with women. This meant men were (or at least acted) strong, capable, dependable; they didn't show weakness, and were resourceful and decisive. These were traits that women were unconsciously attracted to.

Even today women may instinctively be attracted to dominant male traits such as self-confidence, charismatic personality, earning potential, and power. But while women may still be attracted to the security wealth provides, they are now also attracted to traits such as intelligence—or specific types of intelligence—in men. As society has evolved from one of hunting and gathering to one of information transference, intelligence has become a more important commodity in success than physical strength.

The invention of computers and the type of intellectual aptitude required to understand them opened up new avenues of success for many males who previously may not have fit within certain masculine standards. Hence men who even a decade or two ago were considered undesirable to women (physically weaker, less dominant or powerful, etc.)

have suddenly become hot commodities due to their wealth potential. Bill Gates turned the dating world upside down by his model of wealthy nerd success. Physical strength, hardiness, and action-oriented problem-solving solutions were no longer required in order to survive or succeed in life. The new ability to make money and gain status with brains and not brawn changed the playing field for men. As computer geek chic became acceptable to females, a softer, less threatening (perhaps more feminized) version of masculinity has evolved. This transformation has confused other more traditional males who now find themselves trying to adapt to new standards in order to attract women.

One of the things that has changed the most in recent times has been the redefinition of masculinity and how a man interacts in his relationships. Some of this has been really good (most young men today are more openly loving and caring than their counterparts from the past), and some not so good (more men now than ever reproduce and then abandon their families). Either way, men today are a bit confused regarding relationships and their roles and responsibilities within them. Let's look at some of those relationships and determine how a wife can use her powerful gifts to enable her husband to prosper.

Marriage

Love seems the swiftest but it is the slowest of all growths. No man or woman really knows what perfect love is until they have been married a quarter of a century.

—*Mark Twain*

After I spoke at a large inspirational men's conference, an usher approached me. He told me that a young man was still sitting in the seats and was very upset. He suggested someone (me) should go talk to him. Since I'm not a pastor or a trained counselor I am always somewhat anxious about speaking with people who are emotionally upset. But the topics I speak on often touch people deeply, so I feel an obligation to talk with someone whenever there is a need.

Somewhat apprehensively I approached the man and asked if he was okay. Shakily, he told me that the day before the conference his wife had left him, taking their two young daughters with her. He was miserable and disconsolate, his grief having weighed heavily on him the entire weekend. After praying with him, I began talking with him about the struggles he and his wife had been having. Finally I asked him, "How long have you been having problems with your marriage?"

Not surprisingly, he responded as most men do in similar situations. Tearfully he said, "Well *I* thought we had been having problems for about a year, but my wife says we've had trouble for the past eight years." Like most men, he was slightly oblivious to the problems in his marriage relationship. Is it purely ignorance on a man's part, or is it just the desire to avoid anything painful, hoping it will go away on its own? Perhaps because men are taught to ignore physical pain and hardships, they unconsciously approach emotional pain in the same manner.

I have to confess, I dread having discussions with my wife about problems in our relationship. Those kinds of discussions are messy and difficult, and most of the time I end up feeling wrong, regardless of whether I am or not. Discussions like these cause us men to face our deficiencies and character flaws. They force us to stretch and grow areas of our personalities that are not comfortable for us to deal with. Not only that, but most of the time it requires us to admit we were wrong and apologize—not something most men relish doing. Learning to deal with our emotions in a healthy manner is one of the things that causes men to mature. But that process is one that many men are reluctant to engage in, precisely because it is so difficult for us.

It seems to take men a long time to mature, especially regarding relationships. In particular, men from broken or wounded backgrounds struggle in their relationships. I don't think I actually matured until I was in my early forties. That problem is compounded by the fact that young men today mature even later than they did when I was young. For instance, as was common then, I left home on the day I turned eighteen and never looked back. Our son might (would) still be happily living in our home at age twenty-five had I not somewhat forcefully ushered him out the door.

For most of the women I hear from who are struggling in their relationships, the blame for their issues seems to be securely placed on the front porch of the men in their lives. While women don't necessarily make that assertion, from my observations men *are* the problem in most situations. Men tend to be self-centered; they focus on getting their needs met without too much regard for anyone else's. I don't say that to demean men; it's just a fact of life. Whether there are logical reasons for that (which there are) is beside the point. I spend most of my waking hours concerned to one degree or another about how to satisfy my own needs. I don't even consciously think about it, I just run on an autopilot system that seeks to fulfill my needs.

In fact, I'm not sure what women see in men. Frankly, I can be a bit of a jerk from time to time (well, maybe most of the time) yet my wife loves me wholeheartedly and unreservedly. Is this a gift that God has given women to see through the flaws of men and still love them, sometimes to their own detriment? When I come home and she looks at me like I am the only man in the world who matters, it floors me. Do I deserve that loyalty and unconditional love? Probably not—at least not most of the time. I have to admit, men do some pretty stupid stuff. I've said and done things that I knew were a bad idea the minute I did them. It's not that we are dumb. It's just that in hindsight we do stuff that was not a good idea.

Other times women are capable of seeing nothing but a man's mistakes and foibles. I frequently observe that the men who should be judged harshly by their wives are loved most deeply (or their faults overlooked anyway), and the ones who should probably be given some slack are taunted and criticized the most by the women they love.

Probably the role I struggle with most in life is that of being a husband. Certainly it's the role I feel most inadequate for. Being married is just plain hard work. It's not that I don't *want* to be a good husband, or that I don't care; it's more that oftentimes I just don't know what I'm supposed to do. Or maybe I do know what I'm supposed to do but am too lazy or self-centered to do it. Either way, I struggle in this area, and I suspect most other men do as well.

Relational Conflict Resolution

> All men make mistakes, but married men find out about them sooner.
>
> —*Red Skelton*

All relationships have disagreements. How successful relationships are has a lot to do with how those disagreements are resolved.

Here is one woman's advice to a newlywed friend: "I always tell her there are two things you will fight over: money and sex! These are the two areas that I and my friends who are married seem to battle over and over. I don't think I was ever told this and I am trying to prepare my friend for this." Men and women, however, tend to look at disagreements from differing perspectives.

It's been my observation that most women have a tendency to hold on to hurts, slights, and minor wounds for long periods of time. Maybe all women keep some sort of mental balance sheet regarding their husbands' mistakes and things that angered them. I have learned over the years that it takes my wife longer to get over being mad than it does me. Typically, I blow up and forget about it in a short period of time. But she can recall by date, time, and seriousness of offense everything I've ever done to make her mad over the past thirty years with total clarity. I can't even remember the last time I was mad at her, much less what it was about. However, I am blessed that my wife has learned over the years that not everything is a "hanging" offense. Frankly, most of those things were very minor. If you make a war out of everything, then eventually nothing is important because everything is *too* important.

One thing that is helpful is to not dwell on your husband's mistakes; always remember the good things he does as well as the bad. If he works hard to provide, is faithful to his marriage vows, and tries to be a good father, that's a pretty good man. Will he make mistakes and say things he shouldn't? Sure he

Differences: Comments by Men[1]

"If I want to go to bed later than you it doesn't mean I don't love you. It means I want to go to bed later than you."

"When I ask for space it doesn't mean I don't love you or that I'm abandoning you: I just need time to regroup."

"Silence can be a good thing. Just because I'm not talking or 'sharing' all the time doesn't mean there's a problem."

"Just because we go to bed angry every now and then, doesn't mean we are headed for divorce."

[Note: While the Bible does say not to let the sun go down while you are still angry (Eph. 4:26), it may be unrealistic to think that a married couple will never go to bed angry at each other. The challenge is to understand the dangers in allowing anger to fester, while still recognizing that sometimes you need to "sleep" on an issue in order to come to a solution.]

will. He's human and has many faults just like every man. But if you are married to a good man, I promise you he is *trying*. That counts for something. The problem comes when people quit trying—then the relationship has real problems.

Even though most of the time I know we men are wrong in situations, we are not *always* wrong. Understand the value of saying you're sorry when appropriate. Women often get overwhelmed with all the issues in their lives. Bill Farrel says, "Relationships are more complicated because women know those relationships can always be better. There is always something that can be worked on, something that can be done better, something that can be understood better. In response, women will either consistently explore their relationships or get overwhelmed by them and withdraw."[2]

In addition, the time a husband and wife devote to one another determines the quality of their relationship. The stresses of life, whether they are financial, parental, family-related, or work-related, can negatively impact a marriage and lead to unnecessary arguments. Spouses who do not prioritize their time together get caught in the trap of drifting away from one another due to the pressures of life. Here's how one woman described this dilemma:

> As companies are requiring more and more out of their employees (our husbands), their time is being stretched and family is getting the raw end of the deal. In order for our hubbies to get quality time with the children, there is less and less time for us (the wives). This vicious cycle of trying to keep the most important relationship strong and not really having time (or energy) to devote to it is causing so much discord in marriages today. Put all this on the table, add in a woman trying to make it all work (as we always try to do), and we are pulling our hair out trying to do the impossible—which is to satisfy the love of our life and make him happy! All this makes for grumpy mates and no real answers in sight. I can't get enough of my husband's time, and when we do spend time together we are both a little edgy.

One thing I've noticed is that when other areas of a man's life are causing difficulties (such as work), which causes him to focus most of his attention on them in order to solve them, that is the time when a wife often feels neglected and wants to immediately work on resolving the "relationship" problems. The man, being less adept at focusing on several important things at once, is unable to "fix" these problems during this time of great stress, and so their relationship deteriorates even more. As they drift further apart, the woman is compelled to push harder, as it is her nature to ensure her relationships are healthy. But this pushing results in even more stress for the man, causing him to shut down or avoid the pressure. Sometimes it is important to realize that patience is important; not all problems need to be (or can be) resolved this instant.

By her nature a woman needs her relationships to be stable and secure. One woman said, "I've noticed that as time goes on and our children get older and his job gets more demanding, we are traveling in different directions. Needs are changing and I don't like change!" Make it a priority to spend time alone with your spouse. A man needs to know his wife thinks about him on occasions other than when she's upset with him. You'll find that by investing in your marriage and spending time with one another, you'll limit the number of disagreements you have.

Parenting

> Help me be a hero to my kids. Speak well of me and the good things that I do. Don't only speak about my shortcomings.
>
> —*J. S. Salt,* How to Be the Almost Perfect Wife

The quality of your marriage is the single most important factor in raising healthy, well-adjusted children. Husbands and wives who love and respect each other raise children who have healthy values, self-esteem, and good relationship skills.

To accomplish that, consider putting your husband *before* your children. I know that goes against most women's maternal instincts. But your husband was there before your children were born, and he'll be there long after your children have moved on in life. Besides, the kind of importance and respect you place upon your husband affects how your son will feel he should be treated by his wife and how your daughter will expect to treat her husband. If you show contempt toward your husband, your daughter will treat her husband that way and your son will expect his wife to have contempt for him. Your husband needs to occupy the number one spot in your heart. You cannot place your children or your extended family ahead of him in your heart. If you don't put him first, not only will that injure him, but it will destroy your relationship and eventually harm the lives of your children.

Especially when children are young, it is easy for a woman to get into the habit of showering all her attention and love on these precious beings that she nurtured and birthed. These little creatures are so needy and take up so much time and attention, but that guy standing on the sidelines needs to be reassured that he's number one in your heart. Most guys will readily admit that their wives are really great mothers— sometimes too good! Oftentimes men feel like they only get their wife's attention after everyone else (the kids, her parents, the dog) have had their needs met. He gets what's left over after everyone else is taken care of. Just like your kids need to hear "I love you" and "I'm proud of you," your husband also needs to hear those words from you. Even though words generally do not mean as much to males as they do to females, words from the important women in a man's life (his mother, his wife, etc.) have the ability to touch the core of his masculine being.

All dads long to be heroes in the eyes of their children. Unfortunately those opportunities seldom present themselves. My wife was the biggest asset I had in my role as a father. She praised and lifted me up to our children in situations where I could not, garnering me much respect and admiration. She helped me look like a hero in the eyes of our children by emphasizing the important role I played in their lives. The level of respect a wife shows her husband determines how much his children respect him. The love and admiration she has for her husband directly influences how his children see him. It also models a healthy, biblical marriage for them. Make sure you both understand that you are on the same team. Your goal is to raise healthy, happy, godly, productive adults. It generally takes two like-minded parents to achieve that goal.

Friends

Men truly do need time together with other men. A huge myth has been perpetrated upon the men in this country that we are totally self-sufficient and self-reliant—that we don't need anyone else to get by. This myth has been fueled by a number of segments within our culture, including those who despise masculinity, but at its core it is an attack on the family by evil forces. Men who are alone are much easier targets to eliminate. They can be picked off in a number of ways: through adulterous affairs, sexual addictions, drug or alcohol abuse, workaholism, fear, or even apathy, passivity, and complacency. Because men are supposed to be the leaders of their families, if they are removed, their families become vulnerable as well.

Men are starving for relationships with other men. Our culture does not create opportunities for men to bond with or relate to other men. We need other guys to hang around with and goof off with. It relieves the stress and pressures of life. I am so much more relaxed after hunting or camping with my buddies. We also need the accountability friends provide. Our culture portrays successful men as loners, but a man *needs* friends in his life. A man's friends are his lifeline to a long and successful life. Men who stumble through life alone are more apt to be scared, angry, or miserable.

Additionally, for many men there are things they can only talk about with other men. They cannot talk to their wives about them because women have a hard time understanding certain challenges men face. Only another man is able to relate with and understand him. In fact, it would probably be counterproductive to the relationship if a man were to discuss his true feelings about certain subjects with his wife.

Most of all we need other men in our lives for accountability. I can receive instruction and feedback from men I respect much easier than I can from my wife. For instance, if a man I respect tells me, "You're out of line on this issue" or "You need to rethink your attitude on this topic," I am much more open to that advice than I might be if my wife were to say that to me. When we allow other men in our lives it provides accountability that we cannot get from any other source.

All males need other males to help navigate them through life. Even as adults we need other men to help show us the way. We need men in our lives who have been where we are going, who have stumbled where we stumble, who understand the pressures and stresses of being a husband and father, and who know how to deal with those struggles effectively.

The Single Life

My twenty-five-year-old son recently asked me how he would know when the "right" woman came along. After thinking about it, my best advice to him was that this woman would make him want to be a better man. He would feel compelled to accomplish something with his life in order to make her proud of him. She would encourage him to strive for success merely by her presence. He would *want* to work hard and improve himself in order to provide a better life for her. That's not the *romantic* love that most women are attracted to, but it is a *lasting* love for a man. The truth is, when quizzed, most men couldn't name *the* most romantic moment of their marriage if they had a week to think about it. I'm guessing most women could in a heartbeat.

God specifically says it isn't good for men to be alone: "It is not good for the man to be alone. I will make a helper suitable for him" (Gen. 2:18). Clearly, men fare better in life when they have a helpmate, a companion, and a completer by their side.

Single men have higher mortality rates than married men. Men who find themselves single—whether bachelors, widowers, or divorced—do not fare as well as men who are married. Married men are healthier and live longer than single men do, and they are at a much lower risk of stroke.

Married men have a 46 percent lower rate of dying from cardiovascular disease than unmarried men. The death rate and risks of medical problems such as hypertension, heart attacks, and strokes increase for men who are divorced.[3] In fact, single men have mortality rates that are 250 percent higher than married men. Married men also have much better mental health than their single counterparts, and single men engage in an unhealthier lifestyle evidenced in at least one instance by the fact that they consume about twice as much alcohol as married men.[4] Most men in prison are single and most crimes are committed by men who are unmarried.

When a woman's longtime husband dies, she often does not get remarried. Yet the majority of men whose wives die or leave them get remarried within a year. Men do not do well on their own, especially after having had a wife who took care of them.

In the movie *The Boys Are Back*, a widower and his two young sons struggle to get by after his wife dies. In a classic line he describes their situation this way: "It's like *Home Alone*, only there're three of us." The struggles the three males have trying to develop and maintain a healthy nurturing home environment without a woman proved to be incredibly difficult and frustrating for all.

Men are not meant to be alone. They need women in their lives to be complete and to grow. Women have been uniquely created by God to have amazing nurturing and relationship skills. Use those to help your husband develop into the kind of man God created him to be and to have the kind of relationship God envisioned when he created us in his image.

REAL QUESTIONS FROM REAL WOMEN

Q: **What does it take for you to feel "safe" with your wife so that you can share your weak spots with her?**

A: Most men don't like to admit their weaknesses. If a man admits his weaknesses and problems, they become real and he must admit their validity. (That's why many men won't go to the doctor.) However, a man can feel more secure about sharing his weaknesses with his wife if he knows she will not share them with anyone else, and if he trusts she will not use them against him later (like during an argument).

Q: **Another area I'd be interested in is how men see the women they work with. My husband and I have had a discussion about some of the women in his office, and the ones who are on power trips clearly make him angry (as do men on ego/power trips). However, he describes the females as being much more emotional than the men. That made me wonder if the feminine way I'm prone to communicate is a detriment to the men I work with. When a woman works with men, how does she communicate in ways that reinforce competence, professionalism, and the like, but yet doesn't play into some masculine idea of business communication that is not what God created us women to be?**

A: I can't speak for all men but only from my own experiences. Like with men, I have worked with some
women I respected and with some I didn't. It had
nothing to do with their gender as much as it did
their competence. If a woman is competent and capable of doing the job, I believe she garners a man's
respect just as easily as a man does.

Also, you will never hear this spoken of publicly,
but I think sometimes men resent the (perceived
or actual) advantages a woman's minority status has
given her in the workplace. I hear all the time that
women have to work harder in order to be taken seriously, and yet my experience in the workplace tells
me that the expectations on women are frequently
lower than they are on men. (I know, I'm treading
on dangerous ground here—but you asked.) I have
seen situations where women who were not as experienced or qualified were given supervisory or leadership positions over men when they hadn't earned
them in order to fulfill a quota. Likewise, a woman's
gender often gives her advantages over men in the
hiring process itself. I understand the necessity for
some of these regulations, but you must understand
you seldom can have your cake and eat it too. With
the plethora of sexual harassment and other such
laws on the books, communication is difficult. This
has forced changes in the workplace and in the way
males have had to capitulate to those changes. I can
express myself to a man and say things to him that I
could never say to a woman for fear of being accused
of harassment, offending, or (cringe) hurting her

feelings. That double standard makes communication in the office difficult or at least much more complicated. The vast majority of jobs lost in the recent recession were occupied by males (about 80 percent). Does that seem fair? No, but it's something no one is talking about.

four

His Communication

He Doesn't Listen to Me!

I've always thought that living with a woman is like visiting a foreign country where no one speaks English and the signs are all in some strange alphabet that almost looks like English, but not quite. If you want to buy coffee or order dinner or get a seat on the bus, you have to learn a few basic phrases of the local dialect.

—*Joseph Finder,* Power Play[1]

My wife has learned over the years that simpler is better when it comes to communicating with me. For instance, "Watch my purse" is one of the only tasks Suzanne trusts me with in the store or a restaurant. And she always says it twice, as if I've never done it before. Of course, my track record of being preoccupied and not paying attention to what she tells me may have something to do with that. But that simple statement communicates to me all the information I need (or want) to know.

Many women ask me why their husbands (or sons) don't listen to them. My wife says I never listen to her—at least I think that's what she said (ba-dum ching!). One young woman at a recent seminar gave this advice for communicating with your husband: "Just take off your clothes and start talking. He'll pay attention." Wisdom from her experience perhaps, but spoken as only a young woman could. This was met by nervous laughter as many older women in the crowd looked at her apprehensively, as though they had abandoned that strategy years before.

It's not that men don't listen; we just struggle trying to process more than one thing at a time. Since women like to impart a lot of information (and multiple *types* of information), it often causes our brains to overload and shut down. That ability to focus intently on one issue causes us to struggle when attempting to juggle several trains of thought at once. If we are in the middle of processing something and are fed more information, it is difficult to shift gears to the new topic in midstream, so that information tends to slip through the cracks of our minds, never being fully absorbed or even recognized.

Communication Styles

. . . and sometimes she talked at you until it was like being caught in a flock of fluttering birds, nice bluebirds and canaries, but an infinite number of them, twittering forever.

—*Dean Koontz,* What the Night Knows

I'm always very interested in the way my wife's mind works. Her thought process is often a complicated journey down many rabbit trails. The other day she was relating to me about her lunch date with our son, Frank. Because the restaurant was full, they were forced to sit down at a table with a man neither of them knew. For some reason she was trying to remember the name of the stranger (even though it had nothing to do with the story). Not being able to recall his name, she continued on with her story and we went on to other conversations. About forty-five minutes later, during a lull in the conversation, she suddenly yelled, "Eugene!"

Confused (and startled), I said, "What?"

She said, "Eugene. That was the man in the restaurant's name."

Interested, I asked, "How did you remember that?"

"Well, I saw the pink in the sky's sunset. That reminded me of the band Pink Martini. That reminded me of their song, 'Eugene.' And that reminded me of the man in the restaurant!"

Okay . . . sounds simple enough to me.

Additionally, because women are able to read nonverbal cues, such as facial expressions, better than males, they have a distinct advantage with interpersonal communication skills. This skill is often labeled as "women's intuition." Whether this ability is because of superior intuitive skills or just greater emotional recognition, it is still scary to most men. Suzanne has it, and sometimes it's pretty darn spooky. She seems to always know if I've done something wrong—often before I do! She always knows if I'm being evasive, and she can spot a fib from a mile away. She's sort of a mind reader in that regard and it makes me nervous. Regardless, she has different (and vastly superior) communication skills than I do.

Nagging—Anti-communication

Many women use a technique to get their point across that is interpreted by males as nagging. However, it is important for men to understand that what we often perceive as nagging is really just women trying to get their needs met. Understand, though, that most men tend to shut down the minute they think they are being nagged about something. Therefore, nagging (for whatever reason) is generally an unproductive form of communication.

And while a woman's words can strike at the heart of a man's masculinity, sometimes a woman's body language speaks louder than her words. Standing with your arms crossed, a hip stuck out, and tapping your foot speaks volumes about what you are thinking—usually nothing good. A raised eyebrow or rolling of your eyes articulates contempt, scorn, or exasperation pretty clearly. Slamming dishes around the kitchen while cooking or cleaning generally conveys anger and frustration (not that I've ever been subjected to that kind of behavior before).

Author and speaker Bill Farrel writes about the communication differences between men and women, "We [men] find conversations to be strategic, while they [women] find them [to] be recreational. We like to have a single focus on projects, while they like to include all relevant issues and people. We like to simplify things to make them more manageable, while they like to explore things to make them more interesting."[2]

No wonder we have trouble communicating! Women also tell me when they want to impart important information they want to make sure they are understood, so they address an issue from every possible angle so there is no misunderstanding. Most of the time, however, men (and boys) "get it" the first time (if, of course, they are listening). To belabor your point causes them to shut down and become exasperated. It inadvertently sends the message you think they are stupid. Granted, men often do not accomplish a task or respond to a request in the time frame or manner a woman wants. My experience is that there are reasons why I'm not responding as she expects, but for a variety of rational motives (in my mind) I just may not be articulating to my wife. If multiple requests do not get the action you desire, consider calmly asking him for a logical explanation why. Then respect or at least validate his reasoning.

Finally, empower your husband to make his best decision, then walk away from it. To constantly repeat yourself or belabor the point is perceived as nagging. It also tends to overload his mental circuit breakers and causes him to stop listening.

Man Talk

> He couldn't put this in words, of course, for words were tricky things and never meant exactly what they said, or worse, never said exactly what they said, or worse, never said exactly what was meant.
>
> —*Stephen Hunter,* Pale Horse Coming[3]

Don't assume that everything a man says has been carefully thought out before he says it. Likely it hasn't. It's why men are always apologizing—we say things we don't mean because we haven't thought them through carefully in advance. Again, it has to do with the value (or lack of) men attribute to verbal communication. It is also the way our brains work. We cannot process information and emotions as easily or quickly as females can. Thus it is a challenge for us to keep up during a discussion, especially a heated one. Our verbal response in these circumstances is often one of reaction or a defensive posture as opposed to a well-thought-through position.

I saw this illustrated brilliantly on a TV show the other night. During an argument about another subject entirely, a woman said to her husband out of the blue, "I'd like to have children." As her husband stood silently trying to process this bombshell of information, she almost immediately yelled, "Oh great! Silence again!" He then went on to apologize for his insensitivity (really he was apologizing for his being biologically created to be unable to process emotions and information as quickly as she could). The truth is, I could see the gears in his noggin turning as he tried to process an emotional statement like that and figure out an appropriate response. He was at a distinct disadvantage, and his wife was using her superior emotional processing and verbal abilities in a brutal fashion. Because she didn't understand his inability to process quickly, she was frustrated and angry.

Even when a man wants to talk about emotional conflicts, he may not be physically able. Scott Haltzman says, "A man tends to respond to stress with the fight-or-flight reaction: He feels an increase in blood pressure and pulse, and reacts to emotionally charged situations by shutting down verbal communication and narrowing his visual and mental focus. In other words, he loses his communication skills."[4]

One of the frustrations I have is that I cannot always keep up with my wife verbally. For instance, husbands on TV sitcoms always have a glib comeback ready whenever their wives hit them with a zinger or scathing indictment. I usually think of a witty retort about two hours later when it's way too late and my wife's asleep. I've told my wife many times, "Just because you can articulate yourself better than I can, doesn't mean you are always right." She may be right most of the time, but it is still a source of frustration for me. And frustration usually impedes my ability to communicate effectively.

Occasionally (although not as often as she thinks) in my frustration I will say something hurtful to my wife. A week or two later, out of the blue (long after I've long forgotten about it), I will get a note from her saying something like, "I still can't help but feel the sting of your anger at the restaurant." My initial thought regarding this is, "Get over it. We've been married thirty years—you know I'm going to say stuff like that. I always have and no matter how hard I try not to, I probably always will." She should just consider it part of the package deal—the cost of doing business. I don't mean anything by it; I'm generally just blowing off steam. Just let it go in one ear and out the other.

The point is, I am a human male and I make mistakes. No matter how hard I try, I will still become angry, frustrated, rude, or childish from time to time. Yes, my wife probably deserves better. In fact, every night when I pray for my wife as she lies sleeping next to me, I pray that if something should happen to me that God would bring her a better man than I am who would make her happy. I also pray that God would help me to be a better husband and that he would bring my wife happiness and contentment.

Then I usually just suck it up and apologize to make her happy so we can move on.

Share Your Rules

Several years ago I was on a speaking tour of Texas with my wife when what has become known as the infamous "San Antonio Incident" occurred. One day we stopped in downtown San Antonio and stayed at a wonderful hotel across the street from the Alamo. Later that evening we took a leisurely stroll hand in hand and visited the shops along the River Walk. We then shared a romantic candlelit dinner at an outdoor table overlooking the river. As we talked and slowly ate our steaks in the candlelight, I made a mistake that haunts me to this day. I somewhat absently commented that the woman at the table behind me had a nice laugh. I didn't make a big deal of it, just mentioned it in passing. In fact, I couldn't even see her but had been hearing her happy, trilling laughter in the background during the course of our conversation.

Suddenly the air temperature surrounding our table dropped to near arctic levels. I'm still not *exactly* sure why, but my wife was perhaps as mad at me as she has ever been during our previous twenty-eight years of marriage. It was as if I had broken some sacred, unspoken rule that was obvious to all of womankind but that was unknown to me. She stormed off to the hotel with me trailing behind doing damage control as quickly (and lamely) as I could. She fumed at me for the better part of several days afterward. From what I've been able to piece together, I somehow betrayed a sacred rule of womanhood by being peripherally aware of another woman during a time when my entire focus was supposed to be solely on my wife. Needless to say, I might be stupid but I'm not dumb. I've never mentioned another woman's laugh since.

Women have many unspoken rules that they all seem to know but they never share with men until it's too late. The way a woman was raised, the model she observed in her parents' relationship, and the relationship and communication rules in her childhood home all influence the way she internally believes a male and female should relate to one another. Oftentimes these assumptions are diametrically opposed to the modeling and training her husband was exposed to while growing up.

If you have unspoken rules, please let your husband know what they are. He can get in enough trouble on his own without unintentionally violating a rule he wasn't even aware of.

Tips for Effectively Communicating with Men

A woman's words have incredible power to motivate or discourage her husband. My book, *The Man Whisperer*, shows a woman ways to communicate effectively with her husband to help him become the best he can possibly be and have the best marriage possible.

So how can a woman communicate effectively? After all, a man is always the last to know when communication is a problem—probably because his wife never tells him.

I've condensed the advice in that book into several quick and easy tips for effectively communicating with your husband (or son, father, brother, uncle, co-worker, nephew).

Give Him Space

One strategy that works well with men is to tell them something you want their feedback on and then ask them to think about it for a day before answering. Since it takes a man's brain longer to process information, this takes much of the stress and pressure off him to respond immediately—especially to an emotionally charged issue. I often find myself saying no to anything and everything when thrust into the kind of situation that demands an immediate response. I guess I'd rather be cautiously rude than take a chance on being wrong. For instance, if my wife surprises me with an impromptu request to go shopping for home décor, I will probably be less than thrilled. But if she prepares me ahead of time and allows me to mull it over for a day, I might be slightly more enthusiastic. By prepping me ahead of time and telling me something like, "I sure would like your help with this decision," she ensures my cooperation. Interestingly, she always seems to "coincidently" schedule a visit to the hardware store right after her store visit. That makes me happy.

Simplify

Learn to simplify the conversation. If you talk to your man like you do to your girlfriends, he will just stop listening. Most men have relatively short attention spans. If you haven't gotten to the point within thirty seconds or so, his attention will begin to drift. It's not that your man is not interested in you; he's just not interested in all the details. The male brain has developed to solve problems. If we do not perceive a problem after a relatively short period of time, our brains say "There's no problem here" and start looking for one elsewhere.

Speak in sound-bite sentences that convey what you want and what's expected of him. With practice you can become quite adept at this, and the males in your family will appreciate it. For example, if you need something from the garage you might say, "Could you please get my trunk out of the garage before I leave at noon today?" Your husband knows what to do and when—pretty much all the information he needs at this point. If he wants more he will ask. I promise if you volunteer the reason that you need the trunk is because ". . . my great aunt Sarah gave me a dress pattern that her niece wants to copy and make a dress so she can wear it to the county fair in Wichita, Kansas, in order to impress a young man she met from Toledo who is involved in antique dress patterns, and it's in the trunk behind a 1963 copy of *Vanity Fair*, which by the way has a delicious recipe for . . ." he will shut down and begrudge getting the trunk for you.

Also, one of the things I've tried to get across to my wife is only start a conversation when I am in the same room with her. She has a tendency to start talking when I am in another room or walking downstairs. I can hardly follow along when I am standing next to her. I surely can't in a separate part of the house.

One Topic at a Time, Please

Stick to one topic at a time and let a man know when you're changing topics. Perhaps the greatest communication gift my wife has given me and my son is to let us know when she is changing subjects during a conversation. In the past, my wife would cover several different subjects while I was still trying to process the first one. If I was lucky, she would eventually circle around and end up back on the original topic, where I would just be getting up to speed. Unfortunately, I had missed all of the other stuff she had talked about in between. I found this especially confusing if she talked about two people with the same name during the conversation.

Now, she and my daughter have both learned to say "New topic!" when they are switching gears, and it cues us guys to drop the former topic and concentrate on the new one. This is a great relief to the males in our family.

Be Consistent

Consistency is very important when communicating with men. My wife's brother owns a ranch with several horses that my niece rides competitively. During a recent visit, we discussed how he trains his horses. He said that a trainer must do everything the same way, every single time, or it throws the horse off track. Any changes confuse them and cause them to lose focus. Consistency is the key. But he also believes that most horses (like most men) are starved for affection and desperately want to please you. As long as they understand what you want they will go out of their way to please you.

Later that evening I was talking with his wife. She was making pudding for her father. Out of the blue, she made the comment, "I try to keep his schedule and everything he does consistent. As he has gotten older any changes throw him off track." The parallels of these two independent conversations within hours of each other were striking. Women need to be consistent in their behavior with men. If you are inconsistent it throws us off—we don't know what is expected of us.

Sometimes when I ask my wife what's wrong, she says, "Nothing." Because I'm an intelligent, sensitive guy, I know there really is something bothering her. But because I know if I dig deeper I'm going to end up being in trouble about something and that makes me pretty nervous, I back off and mind my own business. And then she gets mad at me for not caring enough to try and help her with whatever's bothering her? That seems pretty inconsistent and confuses me.

Learn His Language

Men are much more literal in their conversations than women are. For instance, when your man asks, "How are you?" and you say, "Fine," you might mean, *There is a problem and if you really loved me you'd stay and ask me more questions.* But he takes you at your word and figures you just need some time to yourself to work through your problems like he would. Likely, he will walk away to honor your request, as he would appreciate you doing. (Also, all men know the word *fine* is really woman code for "the mess is about to hit the fan.")

In direct contrast to how a woman communicates, when you ask a man questions like, "How was work today?" you are probably just trying to stimulate conversation. When he answers with a one-word response, what he's really saying is, "Please leave me alone." If you keep peppering him with questions, he will get up and leave so that he doesn't get mad at you.

Give Him a Problem to Solve

Men love to problem solve and are often able to disassociate themselves emotionally from the issue under those pretenses. You can get much more cooperation from a man if you present your concerns as a problem that you'd like his help solving. Rather than nagging him about an issue that's troubling you, say something like, "Honey, I have a problem that

I'd really like to get your help with." He will be much more willing to address the problem under those circumstances.

Get Physical

Since men are action oriented, they process information more easily by moving or doing something physical. If you want to have a pleasant conversation with your husband, consider going for a walk or a hike, playing a round of golf, or even driving on a deserted highway together (so he's not distracted by traffic).

Physical activity allows a man to process information more easily. It allows his mind to focus on something and be free to listen instead of looking for solutions. It seems to relieve some of the discomfort he feels in face-to-face discussions. You will find he is much more open to having conversations when he is doing something rather than asking him to sit down and talk. Males also draw intimacy from doing things together. The best part of my day is when my wife and I go for our evening walk together. I feel much more free to express myself there than I do within the confines of a closed-in room.

Timing Is Everything

If you bombard your man with complaints the minute he walks in the door from a hard day at work, he likely won't be willing to listen. He needs time to unwind and recharge his batteries. Unfortunately, most women have been anxiously waiting to unload the burdens they have accumulated all day long. Giving him a half hour to change clothes and decompress will often do the trick. When he gets home, say, "Honey, after you get a chance to unwind a little, I'd love to run a few things past you. Let me know when you are ready—no big deal." It's important for him to understand that it's not a big deal. That way he will not be stressed out while he is unwinding.

When your man is watching television (especially sports) or reading the newspaper, it is not a good time to try and engage him. Men do not multitask very well. If you ask him to concentrate on more than one thing at a time, you will likely both end up frustrated. Watching sports on TV is a downtime of release for men—it's a time they recharge their batteries. When I am watching a game on television, my wife will usually say, "When you have a break in the game can you come and see me? I need to get your opinion on something." That prompting allows me to prepare myself mentally for a discussion.

That probably sounds silly to most women, but men do not transition into a talking mode as easily as women do. I almost have to psych myself up for a conversation. Sometimes we feel blindsided if we are forced to engage in an important or emotional discussion when we are unprepared. You can use that to your advantage, but keep these two things in mind: (1) when men are caught unawares or unprepared it can be frightening to them, and (2) men often react to fear with anger. Probably neither emotion is the best frame of mind to have an important discussion—and really they're all important, aren't they?

Speak Plainly

Men and women can learn to communicate, but it takes effort and patience from both genders. Help your man understand that verbal communication is an important part of the relationship to you. Let him know up front what you expect of him so you can both relax. Remind him *often* that you just need to be heard, you are not looking for a solution. Tell him that at the beginning of the discussion so he can switch off his problem-solving mode. Say something like, "Honey, I'm really not looking for a solution to this issue, I just need to talk about it so I can process it. Thank you for listening to me—it really makes me feel loved." Also, communicate to him that when he shares his thoughts and feelings with you it makes you feel closer to him. A good way to help him understand how important this is to you is to equate it to a form of sexual foreplay. That will probably help him understand the importance of talking and sharing.

Speak plainly to your man. Men are poor mind readers, and for all practical purposes they aren't able to read between the lines very well either. If you hint around a subject hoping he will get it on his own, you are setting yourself up for disappointment. Men hate trying to guess what you want, or worse, what is wrong. Tell him up front and directly what you want and how you feel. He doesn't need all the details and who said what. Consider taking a journalistic approach—tell him who, what, where, and why in the first paragraph. Then, while you give him all the details that are important to you (but not to him), he can be processing the key information. When you're done with the details, he should have been able to process the key information and will be ready to respond.

Women like to drop subtle hints, but men as a rule aren't very subtle. Sometimes you need to be blunt. Asking a man if he notices anything different after you've gotten your hair cut and styled is setting him up for failure. A better approach is to ask him how your new hairstyle makes you look. At least he knows how he's supposed to answer that question.

Most men are more than willing to do whatever will make you happy if you are direct with them so they know what is expected.

Why Men Can't Ever Win an Argument

One of the major laws of the universe is that a man will never win an argument with a woman. Even when we know we are right, we always seem to slink off feeling defeated. Not

How Wikipedia Defines a Physical Law

- True, at least within their regime of validity. By definition, there have never been repeatable contradicting observations.
- Universal. They appear to apply everywhere in the universe.
- Simple. They are typically expressed in terms of a single mathematical equation.
- Absolute. Nothing in the universe appears to affect them.
- Stable. Unchanged since first discovered.
- Omnipotent. Everything in the universe apparently must comply with them.[5]

to mention the obligatory apology that all men must offer afterwards.

Wikipedia's description seems to support my theory that "women always win arguments" is a physical law of nature: it's a true fact, it applies everywhere in the universe, it is a simple concept, it is absolute, it has never changed since the beginning of time, and everything in the universe must comply with this law. Hey, I just discovered another law of nature using Johnsonian Physics—Johnson's Theory of Female Argumentative Mandates!

Men and women argue differently. You cannot take to heart much of what a man verbalizes when he is upset. He doesn't think about what comes out of his mouth, especially in the heat of the moment. Unfortunately for men, women do. Frank Pittman says it this way in his book *Man Enough*: "When we men have any important message to deliver, we deliver it as logically and unemotionally as possible. We know that what we say when we're angry should be ignored, and our friends do us the favor of ignoring it. We often wish women would do the same."[6] Women typically think about what they say—and then think a lot about what is said to them. Men often do not, and as a result they say things they do not mean and later regret.[7]

Again, because women are so much more proficient verbally, they have a big advantage in arguments. Most men do not like verbal confrontations—we know we are doomed to lose any verbal argument with a female. A woman who uses that advantage ruthlessly to win an argument no matter the cost is a great source of frustration to a man. It would be like him physically intimidating you with his greater size every time he wanted to make a point. If you've ever experienced that, you know how scary it can be. A woman's sharp tongue can be just as scary to a man as his dominant physical strength is to her.

A woman's tongue has great power, and with great power comes great responsibility. Learn the self-discipline to control your tongue. Don't be a spoiled, spiteful, narcissistic little child like Scarlett O'Hara, manipulating everyone around her for her own benefit and self-gratification.

My wife tells me that women have a lot of internal dialogue that goes on in their heads. That's why they get upset and angry about things that a man often doesn't even know he's done. They stew about little things that pile up and eventually fester. I can tell you that, at least from my experience, men do not have a lot of internal dialogue. What you see is usually what you get. But sometimes still waters run deep.

A woman needs to understand that a man is not likely to open his heart to anyone, but will occasionally open it to one person in the world—his wife. That is a huge responsibility and needs to be taken seriously. Gary and Barbara Rosberg explain it like this: "A man's heart is a precious and private thing. A man is less likely than a woman to bare his soul or communicate every thought. His heart is often locked up and protected, a great treasure stored in a secure vault. The inner wealth represents the core of a man's whole being, the hub of all his activity, his identity as a man."[8]

Women who understand how to use their superior verbal proficiency to communicate effectively with males provide a huge blessing to their family and their marriage. They are treasured by the men in their lives.

~~~~~

REAL QUESTIONS FROM REAL WOMEN

Q: How can a woman engage a man in conversation without having it be a one-sided conversation or, worse, one where he patronizes her but is bored by it?

A: Great question. Any time a woman gets emotional or rambles on without getting to the point, a man tends to tune her out. Asking a man his opinion will involve him in the discussion and guarantee that he will think you are intelligent. If you want to converse with a man as an equal, have a destination in mind for the conversation. Men talk to communicate information, not to bond like women do. Ambiguity and talking for the sake of talking are disdainful to most men.

Q: How can I prompt a guy to realize and *act* on the need for more in-depth conversations without being a nag or being too serious? Oftentimes, it seems to backfire when I try and keep the conversation light and am not clear about my desire to hear certain things from him.

A: Remember, most men are literal. If you hint around about your needs he will probably not catch on. If you need to hear him say something, be specific about your needs. He'll appreciate your honesty and forthrightness. Don't nag, just be matter-of-fact and then let it go. Men also learn best through object lessons. If he's not getting what you are saying to him, wait until a situation comes along that causes *him* frustration and share how that relates to your experience. Or better yet, the next time he does engage in intimate conversation, make sure the reward is memorable—then make sure he knows why he got rewarded. Positive feedback always works better than negative feedback.

Q: Do men enjoy listening to women talk?

A: No.

Q: Do men tend to tune out most things women say?

A: Yes.

Q: Why don't you ever get the whole story?

A: Because it takes too long and my head starts hurting trying to keep track of all those details.

five

His Work

Food for a Man's Soul

Men don't "escape" to work, they go because they *need* to work. When they feel good about their work, they feel better about everything else including themselves and their relationships.

—*J. S. Salt,* How to Be the Almost Perfect Wife

When I wore a younger man's clothes I worked as a manager at a large fruit processing facility. I had just been asked to leave my former position as a plant manager at a manufacturing facility, and with a pregnant wife and one small child in tow I was forced to accept whatever I could get. To complicate matters, our baby was soon born with health issues that required multiple operations. This job had good health insurance benefits and it paid well, so it seemed like a no-brainer to take it. In fact, it seemed like a blessing.

The owner of the company was a charismatic man with a thick brogue. He made many promises about where a young man with my abilities could go within the company and how bright my future was. Little did I know what was to come.

The job initially seemed easy enough. However, once the "season" began I was relegated to the night shift where I worked ninety-six hours a week, seven days a week for about eight months out of the year. The owner was loved by the employees because he never spoke ill to them, but he continuously ranted and abused the managers with unrealistic expectations and demeaning screaming tirades—all in front of the workers. Of course, that did not help to promote respect for management among the employees nor did it do much for the morale of the facility. The owner was not so affectionately nicknamed "Der Führer" by his managers. It was no wonder that the turnover rate for managers was about 90 percent a year.

Working that hard for that many hours a day in adverse conditions eventually took its toll on me physically, mentally, and emotionally. For two years all I did was work, sleep, and eat. My wife began complaining that I had a gray pallor and was dying before her eyes. I never saw my children, and when I did I was too tired to play with them. She eventually insisted I quit. But I lasted long enough to provide the operations my child needed, and I provided a good income for my family. I felt good about that because that's what a man does.

A Man and His Work

I'm not sure that most women really understand or recognize the importance a man's work plays in his life. His work is a fundamental part of who he is and often determines at least a portion of his self-image and self-esteem. A man was meant to work—it's part of his makeup. It's how God designed him. Genesis 2:15 says, "The LORD God took the man and put him in the Garden of Eden to work it and take care of it." Clearly, God knew man needed something to keep himself occupied and that work was what would satisfy him most.

God not only gave man work to enjoy and to keep him occupied but also compelled him to work for all time. God's curse when Adam fell from grace was that he be forced to work hard to feed himself and his family: "Cursed is the ground because of you; through painful toil you will eat food from it all the days of your life. It will produce thorns and thistles for you, and you will eat the plants of the field. By the sweat of your brow you will eat your food until you return to the ground, since from it you were taken; for dust you are and to dust you will return" (Gen. 3:17–19). Hence work is at the same time enjoyable and a bane to many men. They derive both satisfaction and frustration from their work.

Men who have a healthy masculinity enjoy accomplishing something by the sweat of their brow—it develops their self-esteem. It makes them feel like men. It makes them feel powerful to be depended upon provisionally.

Men have been called by God to provide for those under their care. Paul says, "But if anyone does not provide for his own, and especially for those of his household, he has denied the faith and is worse than an unbeliever" (1 Tim. 5:8 NKJV). Because God created him this way, a man may feel like he is showering his wife with love by working long and hard. A woman can inadvertently sabotage his heart in this area by complaining. For instance, when she grouses and complains about how much he works—that she doesn't feel like he loves her because he's gone so much—he is genuinely confused. The truth is, he is working hard precisely *because* he loves her so much.

Unfortunately, a man's role as provider is not as important today as it was for thousands of years. His primary role in life has been eroded because now women are providers as well. That means many do not get the satisfaction and appreciation that they crave by working to provide for their families. In the past men solved problems by working harder. Now when a man throws himself into his work he compounds the problem by being away from his family, often exacerbating the problem.

Strong Work Ethic[1]

Many women I've spoken with over the years have been involved with men who either did not hold steady employment, or else expected to be taken care of by the women in their lives. Men who have been raised by a mother who did everything for them are often content to allow women to take care of them for the rest of their lives. Other men derive great satisfaction from their work and spend a significant portion of their lives at work.

Of course, men need to find a balance between work and family. It's tempting for a man to get absorbed in his work because it's easier and safer for him than facing and managing the many aspects of a relationship. And young men especially get caught up in the desire to make their mark on the world. Understand, however, that providing for his family is one of the fundamental drives that God has placed within a healthy man.

If you are married to a man who works hard and you are unhappy about it, recognize that there are many single moms out there who would give anything to be in your position, with a man who loves her enough to work hard to provide for her and her children. This issue, like many in life, is all about your perspective.

One way to help a man put work into perspective is to help him understand that you are completely satisfied with the level of income he provides. Another way is to help him realize how important his physical presence is to you and the children. If both those fail, call him and tell him you've been thinking about him all day, the kids are at your mother's, and you can't wait until he gets home. If you do that a few times he'll start looking forward to coming home more often.

One of the real disservices we do to our boys is to not teach them the value of hard work. They learn best under the guidance of a father or other older males. I believe that a significant portion of a male's identity is created from the very act of work and (healthy or not) from the type of occupation he holds. Males develop confidence and competence (which define their self-esteem) by accomplishing masculine chores that increase their skills and abilities. Men are competitive because of our need to perform, and we often define ourselves and our manhood through our performance.

Males are physical beings. We process information more easily when we move, we develop self-esteem through accomplishments, we express artistic creativity, and we channel aggression into healthy physical activities. Without the chores and hard work that used to be necessary in order to survive, young males today are turning more toward sedentary activities that keep them from becoming powerful physically, which in turn contributes negatively to their emotional and mental health.

Provider[2]

Providing for women and children is one of the earliest and most basic roles that men have fulfilled. For most of human history, it was the man's role to hunt and provide sustenance for his family. After hunter-gatherers phased out, men farmed the land, and after the industrial revolution they went to work in factories—but always under the umbrella of providing. This role is ingrained in us as men, to the point that if we do not provide it can affect us in profound ways. But sometimes providing consists of more than just working longer or harder.

I owned a relatively successful business for sixteen years before going into full-time ministry. A year and a half into the ministry, finances became a challenge—a real challenge! It meant having to step out in faith for God's daily provision, which was definitely a growth experience for me and my wife. It nearly stretched me beyond what I was capable of enduring. To support ourselves until revenue began coming in, we spent all of our savings, investments, and retirement accounts—a lifetime of work invested in a dream that was my vision. This was probably not as difficult for me as it was for my wife. As a man it probably would not have been as hard on me to lose our home and live in a shack in pursuit of my dreams, but my wife had raised a family in the security of our home. During this time of walking in faith she had to rely on my vision alone, while I was convinced beyond a shadow of a doubt that God was calling me to this ministry and that he would provide.

In fact, I remember my teenage daughter being very concerned when I closed my business and began full-time ministry. She asked, "Daddy, how are we going to make it? What will we do for money?"

I said, "Well, honey, I believe that God will provide for us."

To which she somewhat desperately responded, "But what if he doesn't?"

I told her, "I guess we'll worry about that when the time comes."

After a year and a half, that time had come. We literally were down to nothing. No money, nothing to fall back on. I felt like I was not fulfilling my role as a man to provide for my family. Even though God was meeting our needs on a day-to-day basis, it was very stressful, and if I'm truthful, a little humiliating.

One day the thought popped into my head, "You know . . . you have a big life insurance policy. But you are not currently making much money. The truth is you are worth more dead than alive."

The more I thought about that the more it started to ring true. It seemed to become an obsessive thought over the next several weeks. Perhaps I *was* worth more dead than alive.

One day after a strenuous "discussion" over finances with Suzanne, we went for a walk together. I finally bolstered my courage and shared with her the thoughts I had been having about being worth more dead than alive.

Suzanne stopped dead in her tracks and started crying. She then shared with me that she had been consumed with thoughts that she was not making me happy. Hence, she was a bad wife and her family would be better off if she were dead.

We both instantly realized where these thoughts were coming from. They were being whispered in our ear by the Evil One. He was attacking us in the area where we were being most effective for God—in our family. He was trying to take us out of the game. And he nearly succeeded.

My obsession with providing for my family in the way *I* thought I should instead of relying on God was very nearly my undoing. While it is a man's responsibility to financially provide for his wife and any children he brings into this world (even if he never gets to see them), God very often has plans that are so much bigger than anything we might be able to see.

I recognize now that the struggles we went through, while perhaps not a test, were designed to grow our faithfulness and to teach us lessons we needed to learn in order to succeed with the ministry. Today we are reaping the benefits of God's blessings for that faithfulness and perseverance. Perhaps the best things to come out of this trial were that my wife's faith in me and my vision was proven, and my faith in God was rewarded for my daughter to see firsthand.

Why Men Work[3]

Most men feel compelled to work as part of their makeup. I have worked hard since the age of twelve, but for the past several years I have made a living by writing books and speaking around the country. I also direct our Better Dads ministry. Because I enjoy what I do so much, it does not feel like actual work. Roofing houses, laying asphalt, or hanging sheetrock—that's work. What I do is fun. Consequently, sometimes I almost feel that I'm being lazy or that I'm taking the easy way out. I find myself spending more hours working so that I don't get accused (even by my own self-recrimination) of slacking off. My wife thinks I spend too much time at my desk, but if I didn't I might feel like I was not fulfilling my role to provide for my family. Especially during the times when we struggle financially (which is often in full-time ministry), if I didn't do everything possible to try and earn an adequate income, I would be guilty of shirking my responsibility. It's a bit complicated, but my point is I feel *compelled* to work, even when I really do need to take some time off. I hate to think what a psychologist might say about that attitude; nevertheless, many men feel that same compunction to work.

Because of the compulsion to identify and validate ourselves through our work (something women generally do not have), wives often misunderstand this drive in their husbands and view it as a negative character trait. Of course, some men do obsess about their work and are distracted at home, not fully engaged in their relationships. This is unhealthy and often is psychologically driven by internal wounds or feelings of inadequacy. A man feels that if he can be successful and make enough money, he will somehow prove to himself and others that he is a man and worthy of respect. In a man's mind, that will make a woman love him more and will lead to a good relationship. That's inaccurate and untrue but nevertheless is how many men unconsciously process the interaction between their work and their self-image.

Other men consciously or even unconsciously spend more time at work than is healthy for their family. They often do this because work is easier than relationships. Work has boundaries and rules that are clearly defined and tell us when we succeed or fail. It is much easier than the ambiguous and more challenging duties of interacting with family and other relationships, which tend to be messier. Men get kudos all the time for their performance at work, but they seldom get a pat on the back for being a good husband or father or friend. Additionally, if things are rough at home, the workplace can be a haven of peace for many men. A man knows how to be competent at his job, something he doesn't always know at home.

Healthy men feel compelled to work—it's almost as if they can't help themselves. In fact, they have a burden to provide that always weighs upon their shoulders. Men who work but are unable to provide adequately often feel frustrated and angered by those circumstances. (Men who couldn't provide for their families during the Great Depression often either killed themselves or ran away to live as hobos rather than face their failure in this area.) They may not always like their job, but they know working is one of their key roles in life and so they accept it. Men who are unable to work at all often suffer from debilitating psychological problems. And men who *choose* not to work often have an unhealthy self-image or self-esteem.

Boys raised with the model of a woman being the only provider in their lives often do not develop this strong sense of duty to provide for their families. Interestingly, a self-proclaimed feminist once criticized one of my books on marriage because of the "stereotype" I used about healthy men being compelled to work. She stated that her husband would never complain about taking time off from work. Upon further questioning, she admitted that her young husband was raised by a single mother and really was not a good provider for the family. Not knowing about or not understanding this key mode in men's lives often leads to frustration and contributes to continuing the cycle of broken families.

A significant challenge for many men is recognizing that even though God created us with a desire to work, he then made it a curse or burden upon us as a consequence of the fall. Confronting Adam after he ate from the Tree of the Knowledge of Good and Evil, God told him that for his entire life he would have to toil painfully and work hard ("by the sweat of your brow") in order to survive (Gen. 3:17–19). Not understanding that concept can give us the illusion that more (work) is better, but in actuality we may just be trying to overcome the curse. When men forget that and place too much emphasis on work, it could also be that they are being influenced and prompted by negative forces. The Evil One, like all great liars, likes to use portions of the truth to deceive us. His goal is to destroy what he hates more than anything else—the image of God as portrayed by a man and woman in marriage. And again, because it is easier for us guys to get gratification through achievements and accomplishments than through relationships, we tend to overdo it, especially if we are feeling inadequate in those interpersonal areas. Spending too much time at work or being preoccupied with work when at home is a trap we fall into that is destructive to us and our relationships.

Now, I actually *like* work and the sense of accomplishment that comes with it. And I wouldn't want to give the impression that men shouldn't work hard. I've met too many women who hitched their wagon to a deadbeat, lazy guy who won't work to provide for her and her children. But like everything in life we need the proper perspective—it is human nature to want to overemphasize whatever things meet our needs. So if working makes us feel good about ourselves, we will likely feel compelled to work all that much more.

Especially for a younger man working to build his career, it is often hard for a wife and family to compete with the emotional stimulus and psychological satisfaction a job or business gives. On the other hand, because it is so tied to his sense of self and value, work can be very stressful when it is not going well. His success at work tells the world a man is competent; he is worthy of the mantle of manhood.

Many men have told me that their work is everything to them. They need to work in order to feel respected, especially by their wife and children. When I first closed my consulting firm and started full-time ministry, I think I initially detected a certain lack of respect from my teen-age son and daughter due to the sudden drop in income. It wasn't obvious disrespect on the surface, but it was definitely there, hidden somewhere deep in their attitudes. And when finances were tough and revenues sagged, I always wondered if I didn't detect just a slight amount of contempt in my wife's attitude as well. It was probably all in my imagination, but it was a genuine fear nonetheless. Could it be that even Christians fall into the trap of, subtly or not so subtly, teaching ourselves and our kids to judge by economic status? Fortunately for me, my wife has now seen enough miracles and changed lives that she knows God is involved, and that overrides any instinctive lack of respect she might formerly have had.

Many men have told me they understand the burden of not supporting their wives as they should. I believe it leads to a subtle but very real disrespect from our wives for us as men (though I also think they'd deny it to the end). It's not a lack of love or an abandonment in any sense—more like a low-grade fever that never makes you sick enough to put you down but hampers you nonetheless. I've found that while the love continues, the unease or shaken confidence a wife feels when her husband is not the hunter-gatherer he should be translates into a subtle loss of respect that may manifest itself later in difficult ways. I don't have an answer for that, other than as men we do what we must to fulfill our obligations and responsibilities as husbands and fathers.

Perhaps the lesson here is that all of us (men and women) need to learn to be content with what we have and with whatever economic level we are at in life. I don't know too many people, whether they are rich or poor, who don't yearn for what they don't have. This discontent is destructive and is at the root of many failed relationships.

Men with a healthy masculinity enjoy accomplishing things by meeting goals—it develops their self-esteem. It makes them feel like a man. It makes them feel powerful to be depended upon provisionally. To be needed is to be alive.

A Woman's Role[4]

> When you tell me you're proud of me it gives me a boost—especially when I'm beating myself up, mad at myself for not being Bill Gates.
>
> —*J. S. Salt,* How to Be the Almost Perfect Wife

How a wife supports her husband's work is very important. Many women complain that their husbands have a preoccupation with work and work-related issues, or that they put work before their family. To help women keep this in perspective, remember that a man who works hard for his family is better than the alternative. Some women have regretfully been saddled with men who did not feel compelled to support their family. Be that as it may, a woman can use her influence either to make a man's work beneficial to him and the family, or to make it a bone of contention between them. One of her roles is to help her husband balance that fine line between work and family.

Too many men *are* defined by their jobs instead of by the truth of who God created them to be. However, we should not be defined by what we do but by who we are in God's economy. Wives have powerful influence in creating a healthy self-image in men. A man works as a gift to himself and as an offering to his wife. Providing for her is one way to honor her and tell her he loves her.

Another area a woman needs to remain cognizant about is her husband's career. Many women aren't sure exactly what their husbands do for a living. They have some vague idea but really don't understand what he does on a daily basis. A woman in one of our workshops told me she had an image of her husband as the goofy, insecure teenage boy from when they had first met. But when she went to his office she was shocked to find out he was actually a high-powered attorney who commanded the respect of hundreds of important people. My own wife has told me how surprised she was when she first visited my engineering firm and saw me interacting as an equal with bank

presidents, attorneys, city officials, and powerful real estate developers on a daily basis. It gave her a new perspective on how her husband was perceived while not in her
presence.

Work is a battle and requires a wife's understanding. The
paycheck is not the most important thing. A wife must use
her intuition and be supportive if the work is affecting her
husband's health and their relationship, or if a job change is
in order. Sometimes a family needs to take on a new standard
of living to allow for a change in jobs and a better quality of
family life. Understand, though, that even if a job is stressful
or harmful to a man's health, he will never take a lower paying position if his wife complains about not having enough
money or material goods. Even if a job change would improve his emotional and physical health, he would see it as
an affront to his manhood to not support his wife in a manner that satisfies her needs as best as he can. He will risk his
health and longevity to try and earn his wife's admiration,
respect, and contentment in this area. A man will literally
work himself to death to give his wife the things she wants.
A woman then can greatly influence how much and what
kind of work a man does.

If you think your husband works too much, take a close
look at the messages you might be sending him. Discontentment sends messages of inadequacy while contentment
projects satisfaction. A wise woman recognizes the difference between those messages and encourages her husband
to make decisions that will benefit him and their relationship
in the long term.

Contrast these two scenarios: Carmen's husband worked
long hours. She longed for more time with him. She felt like

his focus on work meant that he did not care about her. Consequently, she started making subtle hints that she would like him to spend more time at home instead of at work, and while he was home it would be nice if he wasn't always distracted by thinking about work issues. Carmen's husband either didn't hear what she was saying or didn't understand, because he seemed to ignore her requests. As she became more frustrated she began to vocalize her requests more frequently and with greater volume. She tried everything to get her point across, but her husband just seemed to ignore her repeated requests. Even though she felt bad about coming across as a nag, she did not know how else to make him understand her need for intimacy. She also felt that his job was unimportant and did not pay enough to meet all their monthly bills. As her frustration mounted, they began to argue more often and their relationship steadily deteriorated.

Irene's husband also worked long hours. Irene desired more time with him and suggested that he cut back on his work hours. As expected, Irene's husband did not seem to process her request—at least, his actions did not change. Even though she felt frustrated, Irene recognized that nagging or complaining did not seem to work very well and decided to try a new approach. She started doing two things: first, she gave him frequent positive encouragement regarding the level of provision he provided and how much she appreciated all his hard work. Second, she began to express excitement to see him every time he came home from work and let him know how much she loved being with him. After a period of time Irene's husband began working fewer hours and spending more time at home.

As their relationship improved they started sharing their feelings regarding the work situation. Irene's husband eventually confessed that the more she had complained (nagged) about his job, the less time he *wanted* to spend around her. Additionally, as she became more discontented and frustrated, he felt he needed to work harder to earn enough money to make her happy again. In the first scenario, Carmen's husband would never risk leaving his job or working fewer hours if his wife already felt he was not providing adequately.

Two women with the same problem—two very different approaches with differing outcomes. Which one was more effective for both spouses?

Real Questions from Real Women

Q: Why doesn't he want to talk about his work with me when he comes home?

A: For men, work and home are two separate boxes. Especially with stressful occupations (like police officers) great damage can be done to the home life when he is not able to "leave work at work." A man is also often faced with circumstances at work that might feel humiliating to him, and he chooses not to relive them, especially with the woman from whom he most desires respect. If a man is passionate about what he does for a living, he will probably want to share it with his wife. If he hates what he does or is bored with it, he probably won't.

Q: **Should a man seek advice from his wife about his work situation?**

A: Yes, in some circumstances. For instance, anything regarding decisions on whether to stay with a company, take a new position, or transfer should always be discussed. However, there are situations where it may be best for a man not to seek his wife's input. I remember one situation where a man's wife felt his boss was disrespectful to her husband and treated him poorly. She continually nagged him to stand up to his boss and not let himself be pushed around. He finally did stand up to appease her and lost his job. The truth was, the man knew the rules of the game in the workplace and did not feel threatened by his boss's behavior. He also knew he was in a position of pay and responsibility that he probably would not be able to find with another company. All in all he had been quite happy with his work situation, but he felt compelled to accede to his wife's wishes in order to keep her respect. Now he's miserable (and unemployed). Because his wife was not aware of all the interactions and relationships in his workplace, or the importance his job played in his identity as a man, she gave him bad advice.

six

His Sexuality

The Center of His Universe

God gave woman the power of sex.

—*Edwin Louis Cole*

Like most men, I'm of the opinion that there are not many problems in life that can't be solved by a good romp in the hay. Personally, I believe sex can cure illnesses, alleviate depression, solve advanced mathematical equations, and probably stop all wars. Of course, that might be a primarily male perspective, but it's probably true nonetheless. At least from a man's perspective there are not many things more important than sex. Sex not only fulfills a physical need in a man, it also fulfills a psychological and emotional need. In many ways it heals a man the same way food, sleep, and medicine can heal an injured or sick body. Men are intensely physical, and so the physical act of sex plays a big role in their lives.

I know that most women are probably a bit exasperated by all the talk regarding a man's sexual needs. How he can't feel truly loved unless his physical needs are being met, how big a role sex plays in a man's life, how often each day he thinks about sex . . . yada, yada, yada. But God created him that way, so just get over it. (You can take it up with the Big Guy when you see him.) Seriously though, precisely *because* sex is so important to a man's well-being makes it imperative for his wife to understand it in order to complete him fully (and to get her needs met as well). Besides, women enjoy sex nearly as much as men do—they just don't obsess about it quite as much.

It seems like I've talked about sex in one form or another in every book I've written. I'm not sure how much more I know about the subject (at least that will get past my editor). So for this book, let's examine the topic from a slightly different angle.

Regarding sex, what do men really want? A better question (or at least one that's easier to answer) might be, what *don't* men want? Frankly, I can't tell you how to be a sex goddess or even how to satisfy your man's sexual needs. But I can tell you from a man's perspective how most men think about sex and what they most desire from a woman. My challenge is, *how can I describe what sex means to a man so that a woman can understand it?* Since I've never been a woman I cannot make any analogies that would accurately compare or reflect the role it plays in a man's life. However, I'll do my best to describe its meaning and importance for us. Please know that I am not just waxing poetic here—these are accurate and core feelings in a man. So let's roll up our sleeves and get down into the nitty-gritty of a man's sexual psyche (you might want to wear gloves).

His Little Companion

There's one thing that all men have in common their entire lives—it is a man's "little companion." Most of you may think I am referring to his favorite appendage. And while many men do think of their "little friend" affectionately and even as a separate entity (many men name it), I'm referring to his other little companion—sexual desire. Sexual desire (as opposed to lust, which has connotations of sin or even deviancy associated with it that normal sexual response and desire in men does not) is a constant companion for most men. It is an inherent, physical drive that males receive at the onset of puberty and carry around for the rest of their lives.

Sexual desire is the little guy that sits on a man's shoulder and whispers exciting adventures in his ear all day long. This desire is the pressure deep in his gut and the tingling in his lower extremities that signifies a woman is present in the same room (or anywhere within a two-block radius). It makes the molecules in the air more exotic, tantalizing, and spicy. This change in the molecular atmosphere creates a heightened sense of awareness and primal sensory acuity.

It is the continual computer-like, unconscious, physical evaluation of every woman of childbearing age that you see, whether in two or three dimensions. These images are then stored away in subconscious files for easy access and total recall at a moment's notice.

It is the constant yearning (like an itch that is impossible to reach, only more primordial) to relieve that physical and psychological ache through release. This urge is instinctive, but it's also a gluttonous conscious desire, like quickly wolfing down ice cream on a hot day even though you know it will give you a screaming headache. A male praying mantis probably knows he will get his head bitten off afterward, but he still cannot keep from consummating the relationship.

It is the thousands of sights, sounds, and smells that cause a man's mind to instantly shut down from whatever it is doing and drift off into daydreams and fantasies. Even while having a conversation with a woman, a man can be drifting off into these daydreams—this can happen consciously or at an unconscious level (like a stealth computer application running behind the active program). Because every woman is unique and different, every woman is a new adventure. The possibilities are endless—the potential adventures are infinite. It is like being a small child alone and unsupervised in a giant candy store. It is an exciting, guilty, frantic, intoxicating, and tantalizing pleasure all rolled into one. And most men like to play with those "harmless" little fantasies a bit.

Does this all sound a bit perverted or even sinful? Perhaps. But I know from being a man and from working with thousands of other men that this is what even the best, most pure-hearted men of integrity face every day, all day. Biologically, a man cannot stop these urges any more than a woman can stop her menstrual cycle merely by willing it. All that to say, good men learn to control, or at least try their best to manage, these thoughts and impulses and take them captive as much as possible. Part of maturing as a man is not being ruled by our wants and desires—sexual or otherwise. After all, these urges are powerful enough to overcome emotions (like love), good judgment, value systems, morals, and intellectual good sense. The ability to control this and not let it get out of hand requires constant vigilance and often mighty reserves of self-discipline.

What Is Sexy?

Men are all different and each has a differing perspective on what is sexy and what their sexual needs are. But here are a few insights that I think are pretty universal among men.

All men want a woman who wants them. We humans tend to be attracted to people who are attracted to us. When my wife walks up and says to me, "Hi handsome!" she's way more attractive than when she is mad at me, giving me the cold shoulder. A woman's sexual responsiveness is extremely affirming to a man's masculinity.

A woman who is comfortable with her sexuality is rare and so very much appreciated. So many women have been abused or had their sexuality wounded in some way that it is a pleasure to find one who just has a normal perspective on her own sexuality as a woman. A man doesn't want just a body to perform on; he needs a woman who responds to his sexual overtures in a way that affirms his masculine esteem. While most men will not admit it, the most important image their wives reflect back to them is whether or not they are capable of satisfying her sexually. The ability of a man to pleasure his wife in this area is crucial to his self-esteem and confidence. I have been truly blessed that despite having gone through more than her fair share of childhood trauma and abuse, my wife somehow came out of it with a healthy view of her own sexuality. She enjoys sex and is a willing partner. She seems to understand her sexual power and the big role my physical needs play in my life.

Even though men are wired to be sexual pursuers, I also know most men would be overjoyed if their wife initiated sex once in a while. Don't be afraid to suggest or try new things in the bedroom. A woman who is open to talking about and exploring their sexuality together is a great gift to a man. Her occasionally initiating their lovemaking is a sign that she desires him and that he fulfills her needs as a lover—both powerful aphrodisiacs to a man.

Men change as they age. When my daughter was in her late teens she asked me an interesting question: "Dad, when men get older do they think older women are more attractive?" Frankly, I hadn't ever thought about it until she asked me (probably because I didn't consider myself old). But after reflecting upon it for the past couple of years, here is what I have discovered. I frequently speak at the annual MOPS (Mothers of Preschoolers) convention and other women's conferences. Being surrounded by four thousand beautiful young women is certainly an invigorating experience. But I've noticed over the years that as attractive as the young moms are, the more mature "mentor moms" who travel with the groups of MOPS moms are, frankly, a little "hotter" in my opinion. Certainly I wouldn't have thought so as a young man. So I guess the answer to my daughter's question is, "Yes." Or maybe as men mature they just learn to appreciate the innate beauty in *all* women, especially the mature ones.

Sex

A man needs the sexual conquest to prove that he can still do it. . . . It's like having a duel with himself. He has to prove it all the time. We don't have to prove it.

—*Princess Elizabeth of Yugoslavia*

Let's talk a moment about the act of sex and what needs it fulfills within a man. To be wanted physically by a woman is very flattering to a man. Not only is it flattering, but it actually speaks to the core of his masculinity. After all, for thousands of years a man's driving desire or purpose was to reproduce so that his bloodline survived. God commanded us to procreate and populate the earth. He placed that desire within us so that command could be fulfilled. From a purely physical and biological perspective, adult males have a 48- to 72-hour cycle that causes their bodies to crave sexual release through ejaculation.

So if a man's wife is not very interested in him physically (for whatever reason—it isn't necessarily her fault) and some young chippie comes along who shows an interest in him as a man, many men are easily swayed into having these needs fulfilled. Some of it may be due to ego, but much of that need involves the fact that a man cannot feel truly loved if he is not having his physical needs met.

The truth is, when men are getting their needs met in this area their wives are actually more satisfied as well. One woman who responded to my survey said it this way:

> You know, if women just realized how easy it is to become the queen of the world, they would get over themselves and take the time to dress in something sexy, put on a little makeup, and flirt with their man. Men don't just want sex, they need it. They need it like women need a hug when they find out that their best friend has cancer. It's *that* important. It takes such a small percentage of a woman's day to let her man know that he matters. I'll bet the same woman would blame her man if he cheated on her, even though she really was the one who deprived him from something as crucial as oxygen.

Interestingly, now that we're middle-aged, Suzanne says she wishes she would have been more agreeable to or even initiated sex more often as opportunities arose over the years. However, I think I can count on one hand the number of times she actually turned me down during three decades together. So I'm not sure what she's talking about—maybe wishful thinking.

What satisfies men most is when their wives are satisfied. If a man can make his wife excited and satisfy her in bed he will be fulfilled. His desire is to see his wife achieve climax. Achieving orgasm is difficult for some women and takes effort. Tell your husband what you like or don't like in bed. Teach him where to place his hands or lips. Show him what feels good to you. Not only will you benefit but your husband will be much more fulfilled as a man. Trust me, he will not think less of you for your openness and honesty in this area. This might be initially embarrassing for some of you, but better a few moments of embarrassment than a lifetime of sexual frustration. You're also depriving your husband of the joy of knowing he's adequate to satisfy your needs when you don't help him to understand your body.

Many men are not as experienced about the female body as we are led to believe. They have to be taught and shown how to satisfy a woman. Here are some interesting facts to keep in mind according to Sharon Jaynes: "A man usually needs about two to three minutes of stimulation to have an orgasm. A woman needs about ten times that amount. A man's climax generally lasts from 10 to 13 seconds. A woman's lasts from 6 to 60 seconds. The Latin word for clitoris means 'little key.' For the majority of women, stimulation of the clitoris is the key to experiencing orgasm."[1] Many men (while they would never admit it) do not know where a woman's clitoris is located nor how to help a woman become aroused and achieve orgasm. In fact, most of a woman's body is a big mystery to the average male. Help your husband feel good about himself by teaching him how best to satisfy you.

Here's another thing that women need to understand. With most men sex is mental—it's all about imagination. I can get worked up just thinking about stuff with my wife much more than I can by looking at images in a magazine or online. I fantasize about my wife the way a junkie does about his next fix. In fact, I've had to take a break and go track her down several times just while writing this chapter. She probably wonders what in the world I'm doing down here that gets me so worked up.

Because imagination plays such a big role in a man's sex life, he runs the risk of falling into a rut in his married life. A woman who understands his need for mental and imaginative stimulation is a blessing and runs much less risk of having a man who strays to fulfill those fantasies. Have you ever asked your husband what his sexual fantasies are? Have you ever asked him how you can help fulfill them? Maybe you should try—you might be surprised how much you enjoy it! One wise woman who responded to my survey explained it this way: "Women need to understand sex from a man's point of view. For a man, sex with his wife is like conversation is to a woman. Not being intimate with your man or withholding sex is the same as if they stopped talking to you altogether. When women take a step back and realize that it's just *that* simple, and *that* important, they will have relationships that withstand time."

With that understanding comes great power, and of course with great power comes great responsibility.

What Matters

Always wear nice undergarments—trust me, it's important. Purchase nice (i.e., sexy) lingerie—consider it an investment in your marriage. Do this even *after* you have kids and even *after* you become "mature"—it matters.

Wear makeup at least occasionally at home even if you're not leaving the house.

Maintain your appearance. Shave your legs and armpits. Keep your fingernails and toenails groomed (I know it's difficult and seems pointless when small children are around, but it matters). Wear clothes that fit properly.

Make an effort to exercise—it's good for you physically, emotionally, and psychologically. When you feel better about yourself, he will feel better about you too.

Don't feel bad about asking for regular time for yourself. As the primary caregiver for your family, when you take care of yourself, you'll be better able to nurture others.

Don't be afraid to role-play. Costumes and imaginative game playing are fun ways to break the monotony that can occur in a long-term sexual relationship.

The Power of Sex

There are so many things about women that turn men on. Few women realize the power of their sexuality, and those who do often abuse that power. I suspect that power itself can be a bit frightening to young women or to women who have had unhealthy experiences. My daughter seemed a bit frightened when she first understood that men, and not just boys, were eyeing her as a sexual object. Of course, many young women like to toy with that power as they learn (hopefully) to handle it responsibly. I can only imagine the rush a young, beautiful woman gets when she is able to open doors with a smile or cause men to do stupid things just by walking into a room.

A woman's sexual power is strongest *before* she has sex with a man for the first time, and she is at the apex of her sexual power just before a man first engages in the sex act with her. Literally, a man will say or do almost anything when in the throes of passion for the first time with a woman, especially to achieve that goal. I've never understood why so many women discard that power so cavalierly. But that's another book entirely.

Women have tremendous sexual power. What does this power look like? Consider how long it takes when a man stands in the middle of the street before cars stop and let him cross compared to a pretty young woman. You can almost see smoking brake pads and smell burning asbestos the second she puts a dainty toe in the crosswalk as the cars come to a screeching, sudden halt. But women tend to lose their sexual power as they age. For example, a middle-aged, overweight woman standing in the middle of the road does not stop traffic quite as quickly as a young attractive one does—but probably still faster than a man.

Before you get indignant over that statement, I have observed that reaction with both male *and* female drivers. For some reason a young woman's sexual power is effective with both sexes. Advertisers know that and use partially clad images of young women to sell products to both men and women (look at cosmetic advertisements or women's magazine covers sometime). As C. S. Lewis wrote, "The beauty of the female is the root of joy to the female as well as to the male . . ."[2]

This power manifests itself in a number of other ways as well. For example, there are no more than a couple of males on the face of the earth for whom I would hoist a big screen TV up a flight of stairs, but there are not many women for whom I wouldn't gladly do it if they asked me. Not that I would want to have physical sex with all those women, I am just genetically predisposed to want to serve the fairer sex. Likewise, what wife can't get her husband to do almost anything for her just by hinting at a night of passion?

Men have sexual power too, although it does not appear to be nearly as potent as women's. While a woman's sexual power declines with age, a man's appears to increase—at least in the area of marriage. Or as social scientists and economists phrase it, "A woman's value on the marriage market tends to depreciate with time, while her husband's tends to appreciate."[3] Because women are often attracted to power and monetary status, even men who are older or physically unattractive can maintain their sexual power.

Even elderly women have some power just by virtue of their gender. Nearly all males will stop and help a woman in distress regardless of her age or physical appearance. God placed within males the innate desire or compunction to protect and help females—although we have nearly bred (or bled) that trait out of young men today.

But a male's sexual power (outside of relationships) also declines with age. One of the alarming trends as I have gotten older is that I have suddenly become invisible to women under the age of forty years old. Since I've always considered myself at least a moderately attractive man (if I do say so myself), that development has been a bit of a shock to my ego and self-esteem. Women younger than that do not see me when I am standing in front of them. They probably think of me as harmless, if they think of me at all. Here's the truth though: the sexual desire is no less in me at fifty-four years old than it was when I was twenty-four years old (although it is not as frenetic and constant). I wonder if it will still pester me at age seventy-four. Discussions with my father and other elderly men would indicate that it will indeed be a lifelong companion.

As my sexual power has waned with age, I do not command the attention of young women like I used to. For a man (with our fragile egos) that can be a bit troubling. Sometimes younger women will say or do things in front of older males that can be inconsiderate or downright cruel at times. They probably don't realize they're doing it because of that "invisibility" factor. Young women at the gym have been known to strike poses in front of older males as if they are not even present—something they wouldn't do in front of younger (and, in their minds, more sexually dangerous) males.

Therein can be another problem that men face as we age. We wonder, *Can I still attract a younger woman—or any woman?* We hear about midlife crisis in men, which might simply be a man becoming frightened that he can no longer attract young women. He no longer commands sexual attention. If he cannot attract women, he is unable to mate—the biological directive, the age-old compulsion to procreate—and thus his life is worthless and he is no longer necessary.

Combine this with the fact that his physical power (muscles) and strength are fading as he ages, and a man can be tempted to prove he still has "it."

That all sounds somewhat melodramatic, but it's true nevertheless. Without that overwhelming craving to procreate, women seem to understand their sexuality better and to be more content when they lose their sexual power. Perhaps it's even a relief not having to carry the burden of that sexual power around with them anymore. I've heard of middle-age women who lose their husbands to divorce or death and remain celibate, not desiring or missing physical relations the rest of their lives. However, I know of no men who do not still have urges despite their age or circumstances. They may not even be physically able to perform, but the yearning is still there.

Insecurities

Many things make a man feel insecure. Most of them probably revolve around his sexual performance and ability to satisfy a woman. As most of you know, a man is generally very concerned about whether or not his partner is satisfied physically by his performance. There are some men who are only self-focused, but most men are somewhat obsessed with that question ("Was it good for you?").

And as you probably also know by now, most men are at least partially obsessed with the size of their sexual organ. Certainly, there are plenty of theories about men determining the security of their manhood by the size of their member. Women say all the time that size doesn't matter, but I guess men always wonder whether women are lying about that. We men often judge women by their physical attributes, so we're never really sure whether women do the same with men. Interestingly, a recent survey found that only 18 percent of women said they would want their mate to be better endowed, while more than 51 percent of men said they wished they themselves were.[4] A wise woman will always tell her husband he's very well endowed, whether or not he is. It's an area that most men probably have a crippling insecurity about, even if we say we don't.

I didn't come to Christ until I was forty years old. So much of my early adult life was spent in the pursuit of secular endeavors, especially during my younger years. After serving in the military I worked at a nightclub before I began dating my wife. One night my friend and I were casually talking with one of the cocktail waitresses about her recent breakup with her boyfriend. Out of the blue, she venomously sneered that he was too small in "that" area. My buddy and I were aghast and shocked that she would even utter such words out loud. We both mutually agreed that she was one woman neither one of us would *ever* get involved with. Even the risk of having that comment breathed in the same sentence with either of our names (true or not) would have been too much to bear.

Besides being circumspect in commenting (especially negatively) about his sexual prowess and anatomical development, what other things are important to make a man feel like a man? I love it when my wife touches me affectionately in public. Sometimes during church services she will idly massage my neck with one hand or slowly run her fingers through the back of my hair. I know all the men sitting behind me are drooling with envy. We also hold hands during prayer and worship—it creates great intimacy between us. This is not an inappropriate public display of affection; it shows the world that she loves me and is attracted to me. To me it yells, *This is my man and I love him!* Being touched is perhaps not the "love language" of all men, but I suspect most men wouldn't mind the world knowing their wife is attracted to them and can't keep her hands off them. After all, a woman who wouldn't touch him probably doesn't find her husband very attractive.

It is important for couples to maintain a healthy level of physical contact—both in public and in private. It promotes intimacy and makes a man feel needed and wanted. I often watch couples at dinner or sitting next to each other on the couch during Bible study. I am struck by how many couples never show any public display of affection toward each other. It feels like a cold and loveless environment. My wife and I make it a habit to hold hands, hug each other, and look into each others' eyes frequently. Our young adult children still feign disgust about mom and dad's being "frisky" all the time with each other. After years of marriage, physical affection is a habit—either you develop the habit of giving it or you don't. Since men are intensely physical, it makes sense that being touched by their wives would be important to their self-image.

All that to say—men like sex. They like the physicality of it and they like the emotional and psychological relief it brings. Understanding the powerful role sex plays in the life of your husband is one of the keys to creating a healthy, fulfilling marriage relationship. Later on in this book we'll explore the consequences of not understanding or fulfilling that need.

~~~~~

REAL QUESTIONS FROM REAL WOMEN

Q: **Visual is so important to a man, but is the visual that attracts them a worldly view or a godly view? I often find myself looking toward the world's view of success to measure how my husband will respond to me and not asking him. What is or should be sexy, beautiful, and attractive to him?**

A: Great question. Here's the short answer—I don't know. I do know that if a man has his core needs met (sexually, emotionally, psychologically, etc.) it trumps the visual aspects of his perspective. I suspect it is a combination of both. God created men with the desire to be visually excited by the female body, but our culture has distorted or perverted that desire into something defective and corrupted, entirely unrelated to God's original plan. My advice—ask him what he thinks is sexy about you. Work on your strengths and forget about your perceived weaknesses. Don't be ashamed of your body. God created it to excite your husband and it does.

Q: **Does he desire me to fulfill his sexual fantasies?**

A: He dreams passionately that you would even consider fulfilling his sexual fantasies, but he probably won't risk rejection by asking.

Q: Do men wish we looked like supermodels?

A: No, absolutely not . . . except maybe on special occasions . . . alone with him.

Q: Is there ever a time men don't want or think about sex?

A: No.

Q: Will we ever have enough sex to satisfy him?

A: Probably not.

Q: How is it so easy for him to be fighting mad one minute and ready for sex the next?

A: First, men are able to compartmentalize the various areas of their lives so that they do not overlap. Second, males equate sex with love and intimacy, so they consider sexual intercourse to be a bonding (make-up) experience. Third, anger (arguing) produces higher levels of testosterone and activates the adrenal glands, both of which stimulate higher levels of hormones that are also produced during sexual excitement. Besides that, there's not much better than make-up sex.

seven

His Need for Respect and Admiration

The "Other" Center of His Universe

Maybe I understand, some, about having to fight. So you just remember who you are . . . you're the Bulldog of Bergen, and the Pride of New Jersey, you're everybody's hope, and the kids' hero, and you are the champion of my heart, James J. Braddock.

—*Mae Braddock,* Cinderella Man

One of the conundrums I face as a writer is the dichotomy between the selfless ministry work we perform and personal success. Whatever success I hope to achieve as a writer requires a certain amount of self-promotion. In fact, it's difficult to get published today if you do not have a "platform" for promoting yourself. The truth is, I don't really have any desire to be famous as a writer and speaker. I could very happily go about my business in semi-obscurity working with men, women, families, single moms, fatherless boys, and men in prison. Unfortunately, it takes money to do that kind of ministry (not to mention putting food on the table and a roof over our heads). One way to pay for that work is through book sales and speaking fees (or begging for donations, which I am loath to do). But making money through those venues requires me to have at least some amount of exposure and name recognition. The better known I am, the more books I sell and the more speaking engagements I get, which translates into more income for our ministry. For instance, I have never appeared on a TV show or radio program because I was the founder of Better Dads ministry. All of my appearances were because I was Rick Johnson, author of this book or that book. These appearances then allowed me to promote the ministry work we do. Additionally, my success as a writer also garners most of my speaking engagements. So I continually struggle with the concept of self-promotion versus doing altruistic ministry work. In order to earn money to do ministry work I am forced to do at least some amount of self-aggrandizing, whether I like it or not. It's not a particularly comfortable position for me to be in.

However, lest you suppose I'm saintly or entirely altruistic, don't think for a moment I don't derive immense personal pleasure and satisfaction from the recognition and attention I get through my writing and speaking opportunities. I've jumped out of airplanes, rappelled off cliff sides, and parasailed over shark-infested waters. But there is no adrenaline rush quite like that of speaking before hundreds or thousands of people and getting a standing ovation. And there's nothing as gratifying as receiving an email from someone whose life has been changed by something you wrote.

My wife is enormously proud and supportive of the work I do. However, she is slightly less enthusiastic about the prospect of me becoming famous. In fact, she believes it is her role in life to make sure I do not get a fat head due to my dubious celebrity. She refers to what she calls the "Elvis Principle": she believes if Elvis Presley had only had a good woman in his life (like her) he would still be alive and happy today. With all his fame and adulation, Elvis did not have anyone he was accountable to who would speak the truth into his life. Because he did not have anyone to keep him from falling off the deep end, he self-destructed. Hence, it is my wife's mission in life to make sure I do not get too full of myself and self-destruct. While she assures me she doesn't, I sometimes wonder whether she prays that I don't get too successful, which of course would offset my prayers *for* success so that we can pay the monthly mortgage on time for a change.

With that conundrum in mind, let's look at some key areas where a man's wife can either help him to be successful beyond what he could ever be on his own, or hold him back from being the success that God has in store for him.

Respect and Admiration

It is a high honor for a woman to be chosen from among all womankind to be the wife of a good and true man. She is lifted up to be a crowned queen. Her husband's manly love laid at her feet exalts her to the throne of his life. Great power is placed in her hands.

—*J. R. Miller, The Family*

Like a great chef, some women know just how to mix certain special ingredients together so their man turns out like the magnificent main course of a fine dining experience. Two of the main ingredients a man needs from his woman are *respect* and *admiration*. He needs those even more than he does her love. These desires are more subconscious than his physical needs, and when used properly they can be an even more powerful motivating force. If you asked a group of men whether they'd rather live their whole lives being loved but disrespected, or being respected but unloved, most would overwhelmingly choose the latter. For a man, respect from his wife may even be more important than (dare I say it?) sex. Well, maybe not . . . but pretty close!

A man has two mirrors in his life that reflect back his image: his work and his wife. Those mirrors answer important questions about his identity, his worth, and his meaning in life. Both send him strong messages about his manhood. The reflection he receives can make the difference between a life of satisfaction or one of frustration. Here's how Robert Lewis and William Hendricks explain it:

Of the two, you as a woman are the more important over a lifetime in helping your man feel good about himself. Why? Because there are times when his work is just work. And there will be a time when he has no work. But he'll want you to be there, energizing and stabilizing his life. You are his most valuable mirror! How you feel about him, how you look at him, how you smile at him . . . those intense feelings of admiration and respect will resurface as feelings he has for himself later.[1]

A woman can be a huge influence in a man's life, not from the perspective of changing or fixing him, but as an encourager and supporter. There are few things that an authentically masculine man will not attempt to accomplish or endure if he knows he has a supportive wife who believes in him. He will withstand anything life dishes out if he has his wife there to encourage him. He can persevere through defeats and failures with the positive support of his treasured wife. A man whose wife respects him walks proud and confident into the world. In fact, a man often equates respect with love. The more his wife respects him the more he feels loved by her. A man always feels like he is being judged by life. If his wife rates him highly, it doesn't much matter what the rest of the world thinks.

But if a man's wife does not believe in him or does not respect him or is continually dissatisfied, he will feel hopeless with no reason to go forward or attempt any new challenges. He will feel like saying, "What's the point?" He will feel . . . unloved. Unfortunately, if your husband is not getting the kind of affirmation, support, and encouragement he needs at home, he'll probably seek it elsewhere. There are many individuals and businesses out there that prey upon your husband's need to feel good about himself as a man.

Have positive expectations for the man in your life—it empowers him! Speak plainly of your needs and desires, otherwise he will not be able to fulfill them. Your husband has a need to fulfill your desires, and it is very frustrating for him to try doing that when your desires are not known. Most men cannot read minds, and we are notoriously poor at reading between the lines. But we do want to make you happy.

My wife's contentment means the world to me. If she is unhappy and grumbling about her life, I'm pretty miserable—I feel inadequate. But when I hear her humming or singing while doing some simple task around the house, I know she is content and it makes me feel good that I have done my job as a husband. I am validated and empowered as a man.

If a man knows his wife is proud of him, he can withstand a lot of slings and arrows from the rest of the world. That's how important you are. There's much wisdom in the statement, "Behind every great man is a great woman." Being proud of your husband and trusting his judgment are two ways that you can show him you respect him.

Building your husband up in public is another way. Tell people how great he is, both in front of him and when he's not around—brag about him behind his back. A woman who chooses to honor and respect her man in public—even if he doesn't deserve it—lifts both of them up. When you do that, you are not condoning his mistakes; you are inspiring him to a new standard of behavior. Many men reported to me that even if their wives do not build them up to their faces, when they brag about them to others it more than makes up for it. They said that it inspires them to step up to the plate to be good men. Men tend to judge their success in life based on the happiness and respect of their wives. *In most successful marriages, the wife sincerely admires her husband and is not shy about telling him and others about it.*

If you want to see your husband walk tall, say something like, "I'm so proud of you for doing that." If you want to encourage him during times of struggle say, "I admire and respect you so much for all you are doing." Tell him you think he's a good man—he never hears that from anyone else, and it's important. Believe me, he will try his best to get that kind of response from you again. Few men would risk disappointing their wives after hearing statements like that a few times.

My wife tells me that many women complain about their husbands to their friends. This serves to discourage him and frankly reflects poorly on you. As one man told me, "Imagine how deflating that would be to know your wife was complaining about and criticizing you to her friends."

Your man needs respect and admiration from you as much as you need love and honor from him. Men need this from their women not because of our pride, but because secretly most of us feel inadequate. Males have very fragile egos. Even the most competent and self-assured of us (on the outside) secretly feel like impostors who are going to be "found out." When you criticize your husband, or good-naturedly make fun of him (especially in public), or try to control things that he is responsible for, it is interpreted as a sign of disrespect and it humiliates him.

The book of Proverbs says, "An excellent wife is the crown of her husband, but she who causes shame is like rottenness in his bones" (Prov. 12:4 NKJV). Not having confidence in your husband to perform a task or trying to tell him how to do something he is responsible for implies that he is incompetent and causes him shame. Accusing him of being inept (even inadvertently) is as devastating and hurtful to him as it would be to you if he called you fat and ugly.

Men often react with anger when they feel disrespected. If your husband suddenly gets mad about something and you are not sure why he is angry, think about whether you might have unintentionally made him feel disrespected. A wife who continually questions her husband's judgment or tries to tell him how to do everything erodes his self-esteem. Nagging and constantly reminding him are confirmations that you do not trust him. That's one reason men hate to be nagged.

Another thing you want to be really careful about is comparing your husband to other men. Just as it is destructive for a man to compare his wife to another woman, it is a losing battle to compare him with another man. When a man's wife says, "Jennie's husband always goes shopping with her, why can't you?" it makes him want to say, "Why didn't you marry Jennie's husband?"[2] But really it makes him feel disrespected. Men are so competitive that comparing your husband (even obliquely) to other men can cause him to become angry and resentful. If he feels overmatched he may even shut down and quit trying. This is especially true in regards to his work and the income he makes. Complaining about his income is like him complaining about your looks. A woman can do this without even realizing it. That's also why it's extremely important to never criticize him in front of other men— they take it as a sign of weakness if a man's own wife doesn't respect him.

I remember when our children were little that Suzanne was very impressed with how well her friend's husband's business was doing. She talked constantly (in my estimation) about how wonderful he was and how he did this and he did that. My business was young and struggling. Because I couldn't admit my vulnerabilities, I did not mention my pain and anger to her, but it caused a lot of resentment in me that I'm sure impacted our marriage in other areas. Even though we have since talked about that situation and I realize she was not demeaning me by her praise of another man, I suspect I still hold some resentment toward this man even though he was in no way responsible for my feelings. Interestingly, years later she doesn't even remember being particularly impressed by this man, yet it is something I still feel the sting from.

But what if your husband is not behaving in a manner worthy of respect? How should a woman deal with a man she doesn't respect?

What If He Doesn't Deserve Respect?

So how can a woman encourage a man even when his actions are not worthy of respect? Can a woman change a man's behavior through her actions and attitude? And if so, what comes first—her respect or his behavior change?

Many women ask me, "How do I respect my husband when he does not act in ways worthy of respect?" This seems like a perfectly valid question to me. Perhaps it's a matter of perspective.

Respect is a precious gift a woman chooses to give her husband. The best gifts are given because we want to bring joy to someone, not because they earned it. If a man has to earn a woman's respect before she gives it, then it is not a gift—it is feedback. If respect is intrinsic to a man's self-worth and being loved is vital to a woman's well-being, should a woman have to continually *earn* her husband's love before he gives it to her? That would be a pretty dysfunctional relationship. It's the same with respect—if a man has to continually earn it from his wife it becomes a burden and not an energizing gift of love.

A trap many women fall into and that I think our culture encourages is expecting perfection from their husbands *before* giving them respect. To honor your man is a gift you give him and is not based on his performance. Here's what one woman said after attending one of our seminars:

> I have been praying about how to be a better parent and I felt like God put it on my heart that the best gift I could give our children was a stronger marriage. Here is one specific way your seminar helped my parenting and marriage: learning that men need respect as much or more than they need love. I have a tendency to criticize and correct my husband. The Lord had put it on my heart to stop doing this, but I was having a difficult time breaking the habit. As you spoke about this at your workshop, I felt the Spirit chastise me for treating my husband poorly. He never criticizes me! It's been a week now and I have learned to change my thoughts and words. My husband doesn't know you but he thanks you.

I'm not sure how or when my wife started treating me with respect, but I'm pretty sure I was not at a stage in my maturity where I deserved it. I can say with confidence that by her telling (and showing) me she admired and respected me, it inspired me to work all the harder to try and live up to her belief in me. I think all men of character will respond the same way.

A while back, I overheard a woman comment to a group of other women, "Suzanne edifies her husband more than any other woman I've ever met!" I nearly popped the buttons off the front of my shirt when my chest swelled with pride. It certainly motivated me to respond by giving her the love and honor she craves. And when a woman edifies her man in public, you cannot believe how much credibility it gives him. I believe it gives him advantages in many circumstances of life that he might not otherwise have. I'm sure that many people hold me at a higher level of esteem than I deserve because of how my wife speaks about me and treats me in public.

Some women may have lost respect for their husband because of past actions. Others of you may be caught in the vicious cycle of not feeling loved by your husband so you withhold respect from him, which causes him to withhold his love even more, and so on until you both despise each other. By recognizing that your disrespect (intended or not) might cause him to withhold love, you can help stop this cycle before it gets beyond repair. Discussing with your husband that feeling loved is as important to you as feeling respected is to him is a good step in helping understand and fulfill each other's needs.

Here is another dynamic that is important to keep in mind. When a man loves a woman he allows her to see his weaknesses. He seldom lets anyone else have that privilege. Therefore, a wife often sees the "lesser side" of her husband that others don't. In her book, *Women and Sometimes Men*, Florida Scott-Maxwell describes it this way:

> One of the poignant paradoxes in the life of a woman is that when a man comes to her, he so often comes to recover his simple humanity and to rest from being at his best. So a woman frequently has to forego [sic] his better side, taking it frequently on trust as a matter of hearsay, and she accepts his lesser side as her usual experience of him. . . . She longs to see his greatness but she has to meet the claim of his smallness.[3]

While it might not seem like a blessing, the fact that your husband allows you to see a side of him that most people do not see can be a huge compliment.

Support and Appreciation

> I've learned that people will forget what you said, people will forget what you did, but people will never forget how you made them feel.
>
> —*Maya Angelou*

A man needs his wife to be his cheerleader. He needs her to appreciate his sacrifices and his contributions to her life. He needs her to believe that he can accomplish his dreams and goals even if it takes longer than either of them imagined it would. A man needs his wife to lift him up because of his insecurities. While our society expects men to be strong and in control, deep down many men secretly feel insecure. I think most women know that and would like to uplift their husbands in that role. But the question always comes up, "What does that look like in real life?"

One mature woman told me this story: "A young woman I work with asked my advice about an issue which had to do with just letting her husband be the decision-maker in whether they went with a wood stove as they have had before or a pellet stove. I asked her, 'What does your husband think you should do?' She told me and I said, 'Maybe you should just call him and tell him that you want to just agree with him on his decision and then not rag on him later if issues arise.'"

One way a woman can show respect and be supportive is to be content with her husband's financial provision. When a woman is discontent in this area, it tells a man he is failing to provide in the way she had hoped he would. Most men derive at least some of their self-image from their ability to provide for their families. Understand that even if a job is stressful or harmful to a man's health, he will never take a lower-paying position if his wife complains about not having enough money or material goods. Even if a job change would improve his emotional and physical health, he would see it as an affront to his manhood not to support his wife in a manner that satisfies her needs as best as he is able. He will risk his health and longevity to earn his wife's admiration, respect, and contentment in this area. A man will literally work himself to death to give his wife the things she wants.

A woman can greatly influence how much and what kind of work a man does. If you think your husband works too much, take a close look at the messages you might be sending him. Discontentment sends messages of inadequacy, while contentment projects satisfaction. A wise woman recognizes the difference those messages send and encourages her husband to make decisions that benefit him and their relationship in the long run.

If your husband is not admired at your house, where does he go to get the admiration and respect he craves? He goes somewhere else. Some men spend more time at work where they get plenty of "atta boys" for what they do. Some men spend more time on hobbies or other gratifying pursuits. Others have those needs met by their mothers, who tell them how proud they are. Still others are complimented and admired by the women they work with.

Men have a great desire to be appreciated. When they are valued it causes them to want to achieve more. Dr. Willard Harley says, "He thrives on it [appreciation]. Many men who come to me because they had affairs stress that the admiration of their lovers acted as a warm spring breeze in comparison to the arctic cold of their wives' criticism. How can they resist? Don't make your husband go outside your marriage for approval; he needs the perspective your appreciation gives him. That does not mean you have to fake it . . . but [set] up a strategy that builds admiration."[4]

Every man would like a chance to be a hero in the eyes of his wife. Men who get the chance to be a "real-life" hero are truly blessed. Unfortunately, the average guy seldom finds himself in circumstances where he can distinguish himself as a hero. One of my goals in men's ministry is to have the vision and leadership to put men in positions where they have the opportunity to become heroes to their wives and children. Perhaps as a wife your goal should be to find opportunities to appreciate your husband for the good things he does instead of focusing on his negative qualities. He will certainly be happier with that strategy, and after a period of time, so will you.

Following His Leadership

Men have been given a mandate by God to be the leaders of their families. Unfortunately, it's a role most men take on reluctantly, if at all. The complaint I hear most from women is that they wish their husbands would show more leadership within the home. And even though most of those women wouldn't admit it, many of them are resentful of the fact that they are forced to be the leaders at home. On the other hand, some men would like to be the leaders of their families but their wives usurp that role out from under them.

Most men would probably never demand headship of their home. The ones who do will likely provide unhealthy leadership. A wife's willingness to follow her husband's leadership is another gift she gives him through submitting to God's directive. This voluntary submission to follow her husband is not demeaning; in no way does it lower her value or status as a human being. It is actually a noble act of obediently following God's plan. One of the attributes of a good leader is the ability to follow. Certainly God rewards our faithfulness when we follow his directives. And if we follow the roles he has set forth in our relationships, he will bless our marriages as well.

Submission is a touchy subject in our culture today. I could write a whole chapter or even an entire book on the topic. And the idea of submission has many differing applications beyond that of a wife submitting to her husband's leadership, although that part gets all the press. A human being submitting to God's will is one form of submission. Submission to civil authorities is another form. A man (and a husband in particular) submitting to the church's authority, to Scripture, to God, and to the Holy Spirit is still another. And finally a woman submitting to her husband is one that seems particularly galling to many women—perhaps with good reason. Probably no other directive in Scripture has been as misinterpreted and abused as this one.

With that in mind, what does a woman's voluntary submission to her husband's leadership look like? How are these biblical roles in marriage applied to the area of decision making? How does a man feel about this issue?

A husband is first called to love his wife as Christ loved the church. Ephesians 5:25 states, "Husbands love your wives, just as Christ loved the church and gave himself up for her." We know Christ gave his life for the church and had an "agape" or unconditional love for his bride. Therefore, a husband should love his wife in such a way that he puts all her needs ahead of his own. This dedication should be unconditional and sacrificial. So if we paraphrase Ephesians 5:25 by inserting this meaning of agape love, we arrive at something similar to this: "Husbands, purpose and do those things that are best for your wives, whether you like them or not, without regard to the way they treat you, following the example of Christ as he loved the church and gave his life for it." That is the first step in the submission process.

To wives, God then says, "Wives, submit yourselves to your own husbands as you do to the Lord" (Eph. 5:22). This is not a tenet to obey or a suggestion of inferiority, but a gesture of willing acquiescence as an act of submission to God. It is not obedience out of fear or by being controlled or manipulated. It does not mean that a wife blindly follows her husband's directives, nor does it mean that a wife does not have equal input for consideration of her opinions, wants, desires, and needs. Mutual submission to each other (see Eph. 5:21) through Christ means that both partners are equal, but for the sake of God's plan the man is held to a higher level of accountability and thus has veto power and final decision-making authority. But he should always make sure he uses that authority wisely under God's mandates and for the good of his wife and family.

A man generally has the ability to see a bigger picture or vision of life, and he needs to use that for the best interests of his family. There have been times throughout my marriage when I was able to see the future consequences of specific decisions and actions and had to make a decision based on that insight. My decisions didn't always make my wife happy at the time, but thankfully she was able to see the wisdom in my choices at a later date and was grateful I made the decisions I did. Her willingness to follow my decisions in those circumstances (even if she wasn't necessarily excited about them) speaks to her character and obedience to God.

So, in God's plan, a husband is to dedicate himself to his wife and do good for her; and through her submitting to him, she is *allowing* her husband to do good *for* her. Wives who do not submit deprive their husbands of an opportunity to bless them. The Scriptures teach that the husband is the head of the wife (Eph. 5:23), and that the wife is to be subject to her husband in all things (Eph. 5:24). So the husband is responsible for and accountable to God for all decisions that affect his wife. This type of submission by a man is a more extreme expression of devotion than the wife is called upon to make.

That kind of philosophy does not taste very good to society's palate, but I'm pretty sure if most men knew what that mandate truly looked like and how to live up to it, the average woman wouldn't have a problem submitting to their leadership. The problem is that many men have abused that power. Frankly, the onus is on men to fulfill their sacrificial role first. That allows women to more easily fulfill their obligation to follow their husband's headship in leading the family. If a woman knew that every decision her husband made was not selfish or prideful, but was done with her best interests at heart and under accountability to God, I suspect she would be pleased and contented. I know many women who secretly and not-so-secretly wish their husbands would boldly lead their family in this manner.

And yet, because of the curse of the fall, many women struggle with this issue in the home—with good reason. In Genesis 3:16, God says to the woman, "Your desire will be for your husband, and he will rule over you." The word *desire* here probably means an attempt to usurp or control. In other words, the man's headship would be a constant source of irritation to her. One Bible commentary interprets that verse like this: "'You will now have the tendency to dominate your husband, and he will have the tendency to act as a tyrant over you.' Here begins the battle of the sexes. In this scenario each spouse strives for control and neither acts in the best interest of the other. The antidote is the restoration of mutual respect and dignity through Jesus Christ."[5]

This constant struggle eventually wears a man down, causing him to relinquish his role and let his wife have her way. Sharon Jaynes, in her book *Becoming the Woman of His Dreams*, says this about a woman's usurping a man's role as leader: "They [men] know God has called them to be the leader of the home, and yet the struggle to fulfill that call isn't worth the effort and hassle. After years of being shot down, put down, and run over, many men sit down with the remote control in one hand, a drink in the other, and a 'whatever' attitude toward their once exciting and fulfilling marriage."[6]

If you are still skeptical, I encourage you to do a study on the word *submission* and on passages such as Ephesians 5:21–33 and Colossians 3:18–19. I recommend a good place to start is the book *Rocking the Roles: Building a Win-Win Marriage,* by Robert Lewis and William Hendricks.

Operating a healthy and efficient home is difficult if you have two people making decisions who do not have the same goal in mind. While a man should always recognize his wife's wishes and desires, and should value her input, sometimes there are situations where a consensus is not possible but a final decision needs to be made. The best scenario is where a man who is under God's authority and submits to his will makes a wise decision that benefits all.

REAL QUESTIONS FROM REAL WOMEN

Q: **When a man is doing something or approaching something in a way that seems wrong, what is the best way to broach the subject without making him feel disrespected?**

A: Most men don't take direction very well. To avoid the appearance of telling him what to do, avoid using phrases like "you should," "you must," or "you need to." Consider approaching a situation like this: "I'm sure you've already considered this, but can you help me understand why you are doing _____ this way?" The other side to this issue is to remember that just because he doesn't do something the way you would does not make his approach wrong. Finally, if you're convinced he is going off the deep end on a serious issue, find some men he respects to confront him.

Q: **When a women respects a man, how can she best show him she does (especially if she isn't married, so physical contact is not an option)?**

A: The direct approach is probably the best. If you respect a man, tell him you respect him and why. A woman's words are very powerful in either uplifting or destroying a man's confidence. When I think about how women best show me respect, they trust that I know what I am doing without questioning me or giving me advice. Many women have a habit of implying men don't know what they're doing by telling them what they "should" do—unsolicited advice.

Q: **When do compliments seem too much like flattery, or is a man a pretty good judge of sincerity?**

A: You're kidding, right? Have you *ever* seen a man *not* believe a woman when she complimented him? Men are huge suckers when it comes to compliments or flattery from women. They'll believe even the most outlandish stuff. It's why women who work in men's clothing stores make so much money in commissions. Men have a pretty good flattery meter when it comes to other men, but with women? Fuggedaboudit!

eight

His Odds of Meeting
Your Expectations

A two-year-old horse is like a woman. You can't predict what they'll do. They're crazy.

—*Old black man,* Something to Talk About

Over the years I've observed a fundamental difference between cats and dogs. I have owned several dogs that were big enough to kill me if they had wanted to, yet I never feared for my safety around them. Conversely, my wife has kept a number of cats as pets. Even though I fed and watered them regularly, I've never seen a house cat that didn't make me feel as if it would gladly kill me if only it were large enough.

I think sometimes men feel like dogs and view women more like cats. Not that we think a woman would gladly kill a man if given a chance, but we are never quite sure what is going on inside her head. In fact, many men (at least unconsciously) think females, because they are more emotional (and thus from our perspective are often out of control), are a little bit crazy or at least unstable from time to time. There's not a man alive who hasn't felt at least a little uneasy when his woman acts unstable during certain times of the month. That unpredictability and volatility makes us nervous. We never know what to expect. The Lorena Bobbitt incident[1] didn't exactly reassure men as to women's mental state. And my wife telling me that if I ever cheated on her she would "take a cast-iron frying pan to me while I slept" didn't comfort me either. She's just unpredictable enough that I ain't taking no chances.

The truth is your expectations determine the contentment you have in your marriage and your life. That said, a woman's expectations can send mixed messages to the man in her life. If she is not clear *what* she needs and wants and *why* she needs or wants those things, it can be very difficult for a man to understand her or for him to meet those needs. All men I know want to make their women happy; most of the time they just don't have a clue how. The following are some things to think about regarding your expectations as a woman, and how to help the man in your life understand them. Your man will lead a much more comfortable and satisfied life if he can understand how to make you happy and contented.

A Shallow Grave

The majority of husbands remind me of an orangutan trying to play the violin.

—*Honore de Balzac,* The Physiology of Marriage

Women have been given a tremendous power to either motivate or deflate the males in their lives. A woman's words can inspire a man to do things he could never accomplish if she were not by his side whispering in his ear things like "I believe in you" or "I just know God has a plan for our lives." Conversely, a woman's disappointment, resentment, or scorn can be debilitating to a man. It can cause him to shut down and quit trying. It can shatter his self-confidence as a man. Part of effectively using that power is to make your expectations clear to your husband. Since he generates a lot of his self-confidence from having a satisfied wife, meeting your expectations is an important part of having a healthy relationship.

Unfortunately, women frequently have paradoxical expectations of men. On one hand, some women make pathetically poor choices in the men they get involved with. They let these men get away with everything short of murder. On the other hand, women with perfectly good men often have unrealistic expectations that are impossible to live up to. They complain, criticize, and nag them about all their faults and the things they do wrong.

Here's how a female friend of mine described women's expectations:

> I think a lot of wives get disappointed and discouraged because of our own expectations. We expect to have a perfect, fairy-tale, happily-ever-after marriage just like we see in the movies and read in books. We expect to have perfect husbands whose only job is to make us happy. We expect when the kids come along that they will be well behaved and low maintenance. We expect and keep expecting. And a lot of the time we don't even voice these expectations to anyone

but ourselves. So we have this perfect life pictured in our minds and then real life happens! Husbands disappoint us, kids hurt us, and people fail us over and over again. I'm not saying we need to give and give and expect nothing in return; I just don't think there are many resources that tell us how hard and messy life is when you are dealing with human beings! Relationships are hard and lots of people have their own agendas in mind. So to sum this up, I think we as women need to be more open to expressing what we want out of life and our relationships. This is hard stuff to talk about, believe me!

This paradox can make good men feel like they are buried in a shallow grave. No matter how hard they work, the dirt keeps falling back in their face. It makes it so they can't breathe after a while. Women seem to want it all.

Author Danielle Crittenden says of the marriage situation,

I think it's generally true to say that women—no matter how individualistic or ambitious they may be—still wish to marry men who will remain faithful to them, who will be able to support their families, and who will stick by their wives into old age. To find husbands with such qualities, however, seems vastly more difficult than it did a generation ago. This is not only because there is less sexual incentive for a man to tie himself down to one woman. It's also because—as awkward as this may be for women to admit—marriage is not as good a deal for men as it used to be. A generation of wives whose prime concern in marriage is not the care of their families but the anxious protection of their autonomy has brought into being millions of relationships in which the woman is unwilling to do much for the man while expecting much in return.[2]

Ouch! I'm glad she said that and not me.

In contrast, the average male's expectations are generally quite a bit simpler. Most men are content with a reasonably happy and satisfied wife who loves and respects them; kids who are generally well behaved and appreciate them; a peaceful, organized home; a warm meal; and a semi-regular sex life. But to females, contentment seems a much more elusive state to attain.

Contentment

> How can a woman be expected to be happy with a man who insists on treating her as if she were a perfectly normal human being.
>
> —*Oscar Wilde*

A woman's contentment means a lot to a man. But having many reasons to *be* content doesn't necessarily mean that a woman *is* content. One woman told me, "I have to admit, my man is amazing and I love him so much, but I love the Lord more; he blessed me with a man who couldn't be better suited for me and two wonderful, fun, and often challenging kids . . . my life is filled with so much love that I should never complain . . . but I still do because I'm a silly, silly woman!" Even Eve, who had been given everything imaginable to make her content, believed God was holding out on her.

One of the stronger sources of frustration for me as a man and a husband is my wife's occasional (it may seem frequent to me) dissatisfaction. It's not overt. In fact, it's pretty subtle most of the time. But it seems like no matter what chore or project I complete around the house, she is never, ever *completely* satisfied. Despite how much money I spend or how hard I work on a project, she is never totally happy with it—she can always find a flaw. No meal at a restaurant is ever quite perfect. I could spend a fortune hiring the most accomplished artist in the world to paint a mural on our living room wall and she would eventually find something wrong with it. And if I buy something, it is never quite good enough or has some flaw that invalidates its worth, even if just minutely. Of course, she claims she's not dissatisfied, merely pointing out the obvious. But you have no idea how frustrating this is for a man, to never have a woman be completely content and satisfied. And it's not just *my* wife. I hear from men over and over again (if they are being honest) that their wives are not content or satisfied with much of anything. And from talking with other men I realize I am one of the lucky ones! My wife is much more contented and satisfied with life than most wives. Additionally, she is aware of this tendency, and I can see her struggling mightily to overcome it. But it just seems like something she cannot control entirely.

Unfortunately, this sometimes causes a man to close himself off emotionally if he feels like he cannot fulfill his wife's needs or desires. John Eldredge asks the question,

> Why don't men offer what they have to their women? Because we know down in our guts that it won't be enough. There is an emptiness to Eve after the Fall, and no matter how much you pour into her she will never be filled. This is where so many men falter. Either they refuse to give what they can, or they keep pouring and pouring into her and

all the while feel like a failure because she is still needing more. . . . No matter how good a man you are you can never be enough.[3]

Are women just more critical today, or have men throughout history had this trouble? Judging by a number of passages in the book of Proverbs, it appears this has been an age-old problem. In my case, it seems to have gotten worse as my wife has gotten older—at least, I don't remember her being quite so critical or picayune when she was younger. Maybe younger women have lower expectations than older women do, or else I have a shorter memory. Or quite possibly I am just not as good as I once was.

It's not that my wife is ungrateful or unhappy with her life (or naturally unappreciative); she just feels compelled to try and find perfection. I had an epiphany on this subject thanks to my friend, author and speaker Bill Farrel, who wrote about this in his book, *The 10 Best Decisions a Man Can Make*. As he explains, because females are wired to *make things better*, they are not easily satisfied and are continually trying to improve everything in their lives—including their relationships. Bill writes, "Eve showed up in a place [Eden] that was all good, and she made it even better by her presence. And thus began the relentless desire in the heart of women to make things better."[4] In every area of life females believe that things could be improved. Women all believe they can be more beautiful, be better mothers and better friends, serve more people, and make people happier. As Bill explains,

> A young man recently asked me, "Why is it that women refuse to be content?" It's because of the nagging, relentless

realization that she could have done more because things can always be better. Before you are too hard on the females in your life, remind yourself that your sex drive is a nagging relentless presence that creates just as much complication and frustration as her drive to make things better.[5]

The idea that women are less content with their marriages than men are is confirmed by studies showing women file for divorce about two-thirds of the time (66 percent). Women also initiate separation from their spouses more often, and they appear to garner lower benefits from their marriages than men do.[6] Whether women are justified in seeking divorce or separation is beside the point. The fact is they are less satisfied with their marriage and frequently initiate ending it, despite the fact that the consequences of divorce generally put women in worse financial circumstances.

One simple example of a woman never being satisfied relates to my wife's cooking. My wife is a great cook—all you have to do is look at my "svelte" figure to know that. She makes the world's best spaghetti sauce. But occasionally she will add some strange ingredient to it. I'll ask, "Why did you do that?"

Her: "I don't know. I just wanted to see if I could improve it."

Me: "No, you don't understand. Your sauce is great the way it is. Please don't mess around with it."

Her: "Well, I just wanted to see if I could make it even better."

Argh! It makes me want to pull out what little hair I have left. Personally, I think everything she cooks is great just the way it is. And yet she is continually compelled to try and improve it no matter how great it already is. Such is life.

Changing Him

American women expect to find in their husbands a perfection that English women only hope to find in their butlers.

—*W. Somerset Maugham*

This "low-grade fever" of discontentment might explain why women always want to change their men. But the conundrum in a man's mind is that if his wife changes him he wouldn't be the man she married. Why would she want to change someone she fell in love with? Perhaps women settle for a lesser man than they want or need and then hope to change him into what they really desired in the first place. Or perhaps they settle for potential and then figure he is a work in progress. Regardless, this is a source of frustration for men. Accept your husband for the man he is instead of trying to change him into something he's not.

Here's how one man explained it: "Stop trying to control and change us so much. We're not 'diamonds in the rough'— we're men. The same men you fell in love with and married in the first place."[7]

Here's why this bothers men. A man often judges his value and worth as a husband (and a man) based on how content and satisfied his wife is. If I am downstairs in my office and I hear my wife humming or singing to herself as she putters around upstairs, I am immensely satisfied. I feel like I have done my job as a husband and as a man. I feel validated as a man. All men desperately want their wives to be happy. Men often go to great lengths to satisfy the women in their lives.

Also, men mostly hope their wives don't change after they marry them, and yet they frequently do. This leads men to

Why?

(Questions from a real woman about men)

- Why are they slobs?
- Why can't they change the toilet paper roll when they use the last square?
- Why do they drop the soap in the shower and leave it there on the floor?
- Why do they shave over the sink and leave all the nasty clippings everywhere?
- Why do they baby their vehicles/motorcycles, washing and waxing all the time—but don't take care of anything else?
- Why, why, WHY do they go to throw trash in the can and see that is full to the brim and walk away?? OH PLEASE TELL ME WHY!!!!!
- Why can't they do something we (wives) ask of them the first time? If they did, we wouldn't continue asking (aka, nagging).
- Why is it my responsibility to find something he has misplaced?
- Why does he "check out" if I'm telling a story that doesn't apply to him? (I already know the answer to this—women talk too much and use too many words, lol.)
- Why do they think it's okay to scratch themselves in public? If I did that, he would be mortified!

wonder why women want them to change (and possibly makes them more resistant to change). A man enters into marriage with an unspoken contract. He likes the woman he married just the way she is—that's why he selected her of all the possible women walking the earth. In his mind, he made a big sacrifice when he selected her—he willingly chose to limit his sexual activities to just this one woman. So, for example, when a woman gains a lot of weight or lets her looks go after she gets married, she breaks that unspoken contract. In fact, in a recent poll of 70,000 people, nearly half of the men stated they would leave their spouse if she gained too much weight.[8]

Here's another side to this issue. Women who are overtly discontent or unsatisfied rarely respect their men. This leads to them displaying contempt toward their husbands. As we know, respect is one of the core attributes a man needs in order to feel good about himself. Not only that, but this lack of respect snowballs to other areas of life. A man whose wife does not respect him will generally not be respected by other men (and maybe other women, too).

A woman's dissatisfaction often contaminates other areas of her relationship as well. Women wonder why men do not want to complete chores or projects around the house. Perhaps the reason is because no matter how hard they strive, it is never done quite the way it should be to satisfy their wives. I could go to my grave quite happy if just once my wife did not find a flaw or problem with something I had done around the house. Oftentimes when my wife wants something done I will make her tell me exactly *what* she wants and *how* she wants me to do it. I'll then do it her way even if it is less efficient. Just because a man does not do something the way a woman would or in the same time frame does not mean he is doing it wrong—he's just doing it differently.

This general female dissatisfaction also tends to squelch leadership in men. Many women complain to me about the lack of leadership their husbands display in the home. Many of these men are powerful decision makers in the business world, so it's not like they don't have the skills or competence to lead their families as well. So why do they shy away from leading in the home? Why make a decision or take a leadership role if you are just going to be criticized and judged for the choices you make? Many men find it easier to let their wives make the decisions rather than deal with the frustration of being condemned. Of course this frustrates women, but you need to recognize that you cannot have it both ways. Either he leads and you respect that, or you lead and quit complaining about it. Certainly, there is room in a marriage for leadership from both spouses, but oftentimes a wife's unrealistic (in a man's eyes) expectations in this area are daunting to her husband.

Besides all that, to attempt to fix or build something and fail is to . . . well, fail. And failure is unacceptable to most men. To fail is to appear incompetent or incapable, even weak. These are core fears to most men, and they threaten his masculinity. To fail is unmanly in many men's minds. So every time a man attempts something he doesn't know how to do, he risks failure and thus humiliation. Why do you think men do not like to admit they are wrong? Why do you think they are reluctant to ask for directions? Why do they hesitate when tackling repair projects they've never done before? Because on some level they are admitting they failed or are incompetent. This proclivity keeps many men from striving for their dreams or even making attempts at greater success, much less something noble.

Of course, this fear is intensified if a man knows that every time he fails his wife will be there to remind him of exactly *how* he failed. This is interpreted as criticism even if his wife is just trying to help by pointing out how he could have done it "right" (i.e., her way). A wife's unrelenting criticism of her husband can also cause him to become emotionally withdrawn.

Questioning your man's decisions is one way of criticizing him. One wise woman expressed it this way: "One thing is how important it is to discuss decisions but to allow the man to have the last word. Men need to be given the love and support of making decisions, and women should learn to be okay and not nag when it doesn't work out after they have made the decision. It is important to learn to trust your husband's judgment and stop questioning him about everything—especially the small stuff."

The other side to all this is that women (and men) should hold their spouse to realistic expectations. We men would probably never grow were we not "pushed" from time to time. Women can (and should) use that power that God has given them to make effective changes and facilitate growth in the men in their lives. Sometimes that requires a woman to understand what her expectations are before she can impart those to her husband.

All that to say, I don't believe women are intentionally dissatisfied with their lives or relationships. But I do think sometimes they come across that way in their natural pursuit to improve those circumstances. A woman has tremendous God-given power to influence a man's life, positively or negatively. Women who recognize that use their power to lift up the men in their lives to be more than they could ever hope to be. In any case, merely recognizing the potential a woman has toward discontentment may be enough to keep her from falling into this relationship-damaging mentality.

Recognizing the expectations you have for your husband, your marriage, and your life can help you have a healthy perspective on whether they are realistic or not. Once you understand your expectations you can help your husband fulfill them, which will make him happier and more content with the woman he chose to share his life with.

<hr>

Real Questions from Real Women

Q: Should wives push their husbands to keep improving, or should we be supportive of stagnant behavior?

A: Wow—great question! The way your question is phrased would lead me to say keep pushing. But there are many valid and legitimate reasons why a man may not be moving forward in a specific area. Additionally, the *way* a wife pushes her husband has a wide variety of interpretations—some good, some not so good. A woman who uses her power of influence wisely and effectively should naturally see growth in her husband without being intentional or manipulative about it. In addition, I am also a big fan of a husband and wife continually growing *together*.

If you want your husband to grow, you need to grow along with him.

Q: Does he think I expect him to be perfect?

A: Sometimes it seems that way to men. Frankly, most of us never feel like we are able to live up to your expectations.

Q: Do you expect me (the wife) to take care of the children all the time?

A: Well, it probably seems that way, doesn't it? The truth is women are so much better (more well adapted, perhaps?) at taking care of children that men often forget they need a break. Biologically, women have traits that allow them to be much more adept at nurturing children than the average man. That said, we have no real excuse. I apologize for my gender in this area.

Q: Why do you expect me to meet your needs when I don't feel like my needs are getting met?

A: Whew! Tough question again—guilty as charged. Part of it might be that I don't know what your specific needs are (many women seem to expect men to just *know* what they want), and the other part might be that it's frustrating if I do try and you are never satisfied with my efforts. That said, in a healthy relationship, I think both spouses *want* to meet the other's needs. Try telling your husband in a straightforward (don't hint around), well-defined, nonjudgmental manner what your needs are. That will require you to sit down beforehand and truly think about what your *actual* needs are and how best they can be met. Most men want to make their wives happy—they just aren't sure how to do that.

nine

His Emotions

Why He's So Uncomfortable with Them

Saying that men talk about baseball in order to avoid talking about their feelings is the same as saying that women talk about their feelings in order to avoid talking about baseball.

—*Deborah Tannen*

Most men are not very proficient at understanding what emotions they are feeling or why they feel the way they do. Additionally, I don't think most men really know what their needs are at any given moment or even in general. Because men are seldom introspective, they tend not to understand their needs beyond a low level urge of immediate gratification. When asked to describe their overall needs at any given moment, men generally do not have any kind of response, because they've never really thought about it before. They might mention being hungry or thirsty, or if given a little more time something like needing more sex or more respect, but they don't even know what that would look like since they've never really thought deeply about it. During a crisis they might be able to give you some examples, but beyond that the average man tends to take life as it comes. Those who do spend any amount of time in self-examination are often troubled or dealing with severe wounds from the past. It makes me wonder why so many women spend time trying to anticipate and meet needs men don't even have.

That's not to say men are dense or somehow insensitive. They just cannot understand and process their emotions very easily—certainly not as easily as most females. Biologically, males' brains have not evolved to process and understand emotions as effectively and efficiently as females. The male brain is not as proficient in processing emotions as the female brain. Hence, men generally have to think about their emotions (sometimes for a long time) before they can understand what they are actually feeling. Even then they may have trouble identifying a specific emotion, as males generally are not very astute in recognizing and verbalizing their emotional status.

Biological Disadvantages

The male body does not produce as many or as high concentrations of the hormones that contribute to complex social bonding, such as oxytocin, serotonin, and progesterone. The female brain secretes more oxytocin than a male's. This means she has a greater capacity to care for and nurture others. When a female hears a baby cry, her body releases oxytocin, which produces a maternal instinct and causes her to want to hold the baby (which then causes more oxytocin to be released). We all get a warm, fuzzy feeling from watching a video clip of a baby laughing, but women get even more of a bonding "rush" from the hormones it produces.

Even the way a female is wired biologically contributes to this emotional nurturing ability she has. Recent studies conducted at the University of Pennsylvania demonstrate this through MRI brain scans on men and women. Scientists induced stress in the subjects by having them count by 13 backwards from 1,600 as quickly as possible. Imaging showed that while under stress more blood flow went to the prefrontal cortex in men, the area of the brain that induces a "fight or flight" response. In women, more blood flow went to the limbic system of the brain, the area responsible for "tend and befriend" or nurturing behavior.[1]

A woman's senses of touch, hearing, and smell are greater than a man's. She has a greater capacity to want to touch something for longer periods of time, deriving joy from the contact. She is creating an inner world that is much more sense- and contact-laden than a male's.[2]

The female brain, with its larger corpus callosum (a bundle of nerves connecting the two hemispheres of the brain), is better able to process "hard emotive data." This is emotional information that needs to cross between the hemispheres of the brain to be processed and communicated. Two other portions of a woman's brain that deal with emotions are also larger than in a male. Author and psychologist Michael Gurian says, "The frontal lobes of the brain, which handle many social and cognitive functions related to emotional relationships, develop more slowly in the male brain than in the female brain."[3]

The female brain developed and was equipped for taking care of children, requiring the development of emotive skills. In contrast, male brains have developed mainly for hunting and other spatial activities like building and designing. Hunting requires a process of following an object that is moving through space and then trying to strike it with another object such as a rock, spear, or bullet. The same skills are required in sports at which many males excel. Hence, the male hunter brain is more focused on objects and where they fit into the big picture, not on the object's emotions. For instance, the deer is prey to be killed to feed his tribe. Gurian describes these differences this way:

> The male brain does not spend as much time processing the emotional core of a deer, ball, or enemy soldier as we might like. If it did spend a lot of time wondering about the emotions of the object, it would not be as efficient at fulfilling its function, which is in hunting, to gain dominance over and, through dominance, to transform the object into something useful to self and community. The female brain, on the other hand, evolved toward, not away from, processing the emotional core of the object. Constant and intensive child care (as well as hands-on care of sick, elderly, and disadvantaged) propels a brain structure to evolve toward in-depth emotive processing.[4]

Because males' primary occupations revolved around hunting, war, and other protection activities, their brains developed better spatial capacities involving enhanced dimensionality, depth perception, and distance. They were also programmed to de-emphasize emotive and verbal skills and to be less empathetic. It is hard to kill animals for food or an enemy for protection if you care too much about them.[5]

Here are some other insights into the emotional inner world of many men.

How He Expresses His Emotions

Because of the biological disadvantages males have in processing and understanding their emotions, it is often difficult for males to verbally communicate what they are feeling. But many males will express their emotions through their actions. For instance, a man may not always be able to express his regret by saying, "I'm sorry." For men, talk is about hierarchy and one-upmanship. So when a man apologizes, he doesn't look at it as a way of bonding (as a female does); he looks at it as losing stature.[6]

Not only do males have trouble making their right brain talk to their left brain, but most men truly believe that talk is cheap. However, men are designed to solve problems through action. So after doing something wrong a man may express his regret by *doing* something for you, such as washing your car or cleaning the dishes. Men typically believe that their actions speak louder than their words. Additionally, because they are not as proficient verbally, words do not mean as much to a male as they do to a female. Hence, men often find *doing* something as a way of apologizing is easier than *saying* something.

One thing to remember is that even though many husbands are men of few words, often those words are carefully chosen and hold more intent and substance than most women realize. So your husband's words of apology may not be as flowery as your girlfriend's are, but they are probably just as heartfelt and may even require more effort on his part.

What Males Fear[7]

> Fear of self is the greatest of all terrors, the deepest of all dread, the commonest of all mistakes. From it grows failure. Because of it, life is a mockery. Out of it comes despair.
>
> —David Seabury

Understanding a male's emotional life begins with recognizing the factors that cause him fear. Fear is one of the biggest motivators of human beings, especially males. Understanding what males are fundamentally afraid of can give us insight into their psyche and help develop strategies to compensate for and overcome those issues.

Over the years many men have shared their fears with me. All males have certain fears that are strong within them, regardless of age. These fears are probably similar in some ways to fears that women have, but I've observed that these particular fears seem to be intensified in males. The following are fears that most males seem to have in common. They might not always be spoken, but they linger within the hidden consciousness of a man.

Males have a great fear of being inadequate. Whether accurate or not, to feel and be perceived as inadequate is emasculating to a man. To be incompetent is just as bad, as it means he lacks the skill or ability to perform up to expectations. As men get older this anxiety manifests itself in areas such as fear of not being able to perform sexually, of being rejected by women, and of not being able to provide financially and materially. Performance is important to males as this is how their self-esteem is developed. Males develop self-esteem through their accomplishments, while women typically develop theirs through relationships with others. This is why years of "telling" boys how good they are (whether they earned it through their accomplishments or not) has been such a dismal failure in creating healthy male self-esteem.

Because failing or appearing inadequate is one of a man's greatest fears, not understanding how to fulfill his responsibilities can cause a male to walk away or never even try if he thinks he will fail. I once spoke to a man from South Korea who told me they had a very high rate of fatherlessness. When I asked him why, he said, "Because our economy is struggling and there is a high unemployment rate. Men would rather abandon their families than face the humiliation of not being able to provide for them." I don't think that is a cultural phenomenon unique to South Korea.

For most men fighting can be a little intimidating because the average guy has never been trained how to fight. But once he gets some training in hand-to-hand combat, either through the military or things like boxing lessons or martial arts, this fear and intimidation goes away. He becomes confident in his ability to perform the task at hand.

Nearly anything that a man attempts but has no experience in has the potential to make him look foolish. It's one reason why most men don't like dancing. Dancing is like fighting—most men have never been taught how. The average guy has no idea how to dance. So asking him to take you out on the dance floor and trip the light fantastic is akin to asking him to step into the ring with Mike Tyson. It's just as intimidating and frightening. He knows everybody will be watching him perform (incompetently) and it soon becomes every man's worst nightmare—failing in public and looking like a fool.

All males fear failure. To fail is to be branded inadequate or incompetent. While men fear failure, it's not as bad as being inadequate. When men fail we just get back up (hopefully), but being inadequate is humiliating. It means we cannot "cut the mustard" as a man. Men or boys who act overly macho—who push people around—are that way because they are afraid of being inadequate. Bullies are always weak, insecure, and scared. They try to compensate for that by making others afraid, so that everyone feels the same way they do. That way they are just like everyone else—they become "normalized."

Men raised without fathers often experience apprehension about becoming fathers or husbands themselves because they never had those roles modeled for them. They do not feel adequate to those huge and somewhat overwhelming roles. Additionally, they do not understand how a man is supposed to treat a woman (or love her) because that was never modeled for them either.

Males also fear not being respected. Respect is a huge factor in a man's life. Often respect is more affirming to a male than love is. To be disrespected is emasculating and causes humiliation in a male. Humiliation then fuels feelings of inadequacy and incompetence in a never-ending cycle of ego destruction. One way to understand this need is to realize that if a man's wife (or a boy's mother) does not respect him, then few other males will either. This is because men have a hard shell they present to the world to cover their vulnerable underbelly of secretly feeling inadequate and unworthy. The important woman in a man's life is often the only one who ever sees the inside of this shell, and only in glimpses. Mothers often set the tone of respect (and thus self-esteem) that a boy feels about himself and can expect from his wife.

Many males fear losing control. To not be in control is to risk failing and thus be vulnerable to criticism and scorn. This is one reason that emotions are so frightening to men—emotions are powerful and often uncontrollable. Males, with their lack of emotional competency and comprehension, are frightened by the power and wildness of emotions. In fact, most males consider emotions, or at least a strong show of emotions, to be a weakness. We are always slightly embarrassed by strong demonstrations of emotion such as crying, especially in other males.

Males also fear being dominated. It not only smacks of being inadequate but also of being powerless to do anything about it. There are options to being inadequate, such as training yourself to be adequate or even running away. When a man is dominated there are not as many options. To be dominated is to be humiliated. Over the centuries male slaves were dominated to break their spirits. Men know that losing is sometimes inevitable, but being dominated is unbearable. It's one of the reasons pro football has rules against taunting an opponent.

Not being masculine enough is another big fear males have—not being masculine enough means not being considered a man. It is why one of the biggest compliments a man can receive is to be seen as a "man's man." Most guys would rather suffer through any physical pain than not be considered a man—that's why being disrespected by his wife (or mother) is so painful. When the one person (especially a woman) who knows him best treats him with disrespect it is like saying to the world that he is not man enough.

Loss of significance is a big fear for males. Losing your job, being demoted, being ridiculed, or even having a baby or sibling take your place at home are demoralizing and frightening to males. Males who lose their leadership status, fail to achieve a goal, or get fired from a job are demoralized.

Rejection is also very difficult for most males. It keeps us from attempting greatness. The sting of rejection bites deep on a smaller scale too. Not getting the recognition we feel we deserve, being picked last on a team, failing to get a promotion at work, or even being turned down for sex by our wives are subtle stabs to our manhood.

Males need to feel adequate and competent in order to feel good about themselves. A wife can use her feminine influence (which is huge) to help her husband develop the self-confidence and self-esteem that will prevent him from having the fears that hold men back in life.

The Psychology of Male Anger

> Men are like steel: when they lose their temper, they lose their worth.
>
> —*Chuck Norris*

Males are not very adept at understanding their emotions or very comfortable dealing with them. Emotions are powerful and often uncontrollable. That's why many males keep such a tight lid on their emotions—once released they are difficult to predict or control and often result in situations that leave them feeling vulnerable. However, there is one emotion that they are relatively comfortable with: anger.

Anger, for many men, is an old friend, one they call upon in a variety of circumstances. Like all powerful emotions, anger can be used destructively or for good. For instance, anger can be terribly destructive in relationships. After all, *anger* is only one letter away from *danger*. We need only look at the devastation caused to women and children through a man's uncontrolled wrath and anger to know that it can lead to emotional, psychological, and even physical abuse.

Anger produces a physiological arousal in males, creating a state of readiness and heightened awareness. It creates energy that can be directed outward in the form of protection or as a weapon. Anger causes a fight-or-flight response designed to protect us. It is frequently a powerful tool that boys and men use to cover our inadequacies. Oftentimes anger in males is a secondary emotion used to hide underlying emotions such as fear, hurt, or frustration. You'll notice that nearly all males will react with anger when they become overly frustrated or are hurt emotionally.

The surge of adrenaline and associated arousal can be addicting to some males. It gives men strength and power, but not the strength that comes from character and determination. It is the strength of anger and passion. Young males need to be taught how to deal with and control their anger. In order to do that, they must learn to own their anger and identify its source. Then they can learn how to respond to their anger.

Males are more biologically disposed to react with anger in various situations. Scott Haltzman, M.D., says,

> When men sense an argument coming, their body sends signals to the alarm center of the brain, the amygdala, which is responsible for engaging the fight-or-flight response. When this almond-shaped brain organ gets activated, it makes rational thought difficult, and all but the most emergent problem-solving abilities collapse. Sure the amygdala is great for getting a guy to rush through a blazing fire to rescue his family, but it's not so hot for helping him think out how to demonstrate his complex mix of feelings when his wife gives him the silent treatment because he forgot to ask her about her very important job interview. Remember, he's good at showing his emotions through actions, but may be less skilled at describing it with words.[8]

On the other hand anger can be channeled into productive pathways. Anger can be used to motivate a man to achieve more than he might otherwise be able to accomplish. It can be used as a mechanism to encourage perseverance under duress or in grueling circumstances. Many a boy has accomplished some difficult task all because he got angry when someone told him he couldn't succeed. When teased, many boys use anger as motivation to prove their offenders wrong. One method in coaching is to get young men angry in order to motivate them to perform beyond their self-imposed limitations. In fact, many men propel themselves with anger and grit to succeed in life because a father-figure constantly told them they wouldn't amount to anything. Warriors often used anger toward their enemies as motivation to succeed in battle.

Regardless of how it is used, anger is the emotion most familiar to males. Anger is often a secondary emotion males use to cover or mask other emotions. For instance, certain emotions such as fear, anxiety, vulnerability, or distress often produce a feeling of humiliation in males. Humiliation is considered a weakness; remember, for most males showing weakness means being vulnerable and open to criticism. To be vulnerable is an invitation to be attacked. But anger is a defense against attack and may even be used as a weapon to attack others. Very angry men and boys are seldom messed with, even by bullies.

Rather than feeling humiliated by these "unmanly" emotions, many males instinctively and automatically use anger to cover them. Even pain, both physical and psychological, can be covered by anger. Notice how most males react when they hit their thumb with a hammer: they'd rather get mad than cry. Most men also get angry rather than depressed or hysterical when faced with an emotional crisis in a relationship. Again, this is a protective mechanism for their fragile egos—egos that are covering up secretly ingrained feelings of inadequacy and incompetence.

Sometimes anger is even used consciously. I was raised in an alcoholic and abusive home. I can distinctly remember at about the age of twelve when I first discovered that if I just got angry I didn't have to feel that humiliating emotion of being afraid. In typical naive boyhood fashion I told myself, "This is great. I'll never be scared again for the rest of my life!" However, this was foolish as I spent a significant portion of my adult life being angry. Angry because I was really afraid. Angry because I never had a positive male role model show me how a man lives his life and faces his problems in a healthy manner.

Young men who are not taught how a man acts, what his roles are in life, and how to fulfill them adequately and competently are very often angry. They are angry at life and at the world. They take this anger out on others, hoping to hurt them before they themselves are hurt—even if that hurt is just humiliation from their ineptness.

Love

> For it was not into my ear you whispered, but into my heart.
> It was not my lips you kissed, but my soul.
>
> —*Judy Garland*

Love consists of joy and trusting another. To a male, trusting another person means being vulnerable. Love and intimacy require a male to willingly allow himself to be vulnerable, which is against his nature. While boys grow up naturally learning to love their mothers, love is an emotion that males need to understand and see modeled in order to transfer it to another human being. Since visual observation is the primary way most males learn, this is also the best way to teach them about love.

Parents provide the most important role model for a male with regard to love and relationships. Men who come from homes where a healthy marriage existed often talk about how helpful that was to them as an example and a source of strength as they discover their place in the world and settle upon a belief/value system.

Fathers model how a man is supposed to love a woman. Mothers model how a woman responds to a man's love. Loving a woman does not come naturally to most males. Watch the difference in how a young man who grew up with no healthy male role models treats his wife (or, more often, his live-in lover) versus one who grew up with a father who loved his mother.

For instance, a young man who grew up with healthy male role models has learned what it means to sacrifice for his family, while a man without that example will more likely be focused on his own needs and wants. Boys with positive male role models learn the intentionality of love, that love is a decision more than an emotion. They learn that the *actions* of loving a woman produce that feeling within them. They learn that love stays for the long haul and doesn't quit when things are difficult. And they learn that a long-term, loving relationship has cycles of ups and downs that are normal. Boys who don't learn that or who have that lesson short-circuited end up failing to understand the sacrificial nature of love and the rewards that it brings.

To sacrificially give oneself on a daily basis for the good of another is not a natural male trait (although they willingly give their lives for others in war). In fact, the opposite might even be true. I know women look hard to find and hang on to admirable traits in all their men, but for males to be naturally (that is, without modeling or training) loving, kind, gentle, and compassionate is unusual.

Loving a woman is a modeled behavior for a male. Learning to lead his family in a healthy manner is another modeled behavior that boys seldom learn from any other source outside the family unit. The respect that a man shows his wife is the level of respect that their son will think all women deserve. Appreciating the value that a woman brings to a relationship and to the family is another gift that a father or other male role model gives to a boy. Learning to cherish and love a woman in the ways that she needs, not just the ways that he feels more comfortable with, is a lesson that a boy will only get from watching his father every day. Recognizing a woman's more tender heart and the devastation that his words can cause her are things taught to a boy by his father. And perhaps the greatest lesson a father passes along is the ability to admit he is wrong, apologize, and ask for forgiveness—not easy things for most males.

Again, because men are generally not as adept at expressing their emotions verbally, your husband may communicate his love for you through his actions. When he fills your car with gas or changes the oil he is telling you he loves you. That's not the romantic kind of expression most women desire, but understand that a man usually thinks his actions speak louder than words. If your man works hard to provide for your family, stays faithful to his wedding vows, and does not engage in self-indulgent pursuits, he is boldly expressing his love for you for the whole world to see.

REAL QUESTIONS FROM REAL WOMEN

Q: Why doesn't he get jealous when I tell him a guy was hitting on me at the office?

A: Maybe because he trusts you? A man who is jealous of you does not love you more than one who is not jealous. In fact, a jealous man does not love you at all—he wants to possess and control you.

Q: **Why do men not share their feelings then get mad that their wives don't validate how they feel?**

A: Most men are not capable of articulating their feelings and emotions. It doesn't mean they don't have them or get frustrated when they are not validated. However, men need to learn that if they are not willing to share their feelings they cannot expect anyone else to validate them.

ten

His Desires in a Wife

What Qualities Does a Man Seek in a Wife?

A wife of noble character who can find? She is worth far more than rubies.

—Proverbs 31:10

A woman has a tremendous influence in a man's life. But it's important to remember that the *kind* of woman you are determines whether your influence will be positive or negative, and whether you will truly recognize and enjoy the blessings that come from using that influence productively. Some women just seem to lead blessed lives. Their husbands prosper, and their children are healthy and thrive. Others attract stress and strife to their lives like cat hair to cashmere.

In order to use your influence effectively, it is important to recognize what qualities a man looks for in a woman. Again, these are generalizations and not all men will want all these qualities in a woman, but they are fairly universal in their appeal.

Outer Qualities

A man has a need for a woman who is physically attractive. Now don't get all freaked out here. Let's discuss this rationally. I know this topic causes many women to immediately get defensive and shut down. But it's important that you understand this need from the proper perspective.

Regardless of whether you feel comfortable with this subject or not, the truth is a man needs his wife to look attractive. I want to be careful here because this is a sore subject in many households. Many women feel the need to try and compete against unattainable standards set by our culture. Many of you mentioned the frustration of being expected to measure up to the "Barbie" standard. But I think that is an unrealistic expectation that women not only put on themselves but also place upon their husbands. Look at it this way—did you look like Barbie when your husband married you? Probably not, so he probably doesn't expect you to look like Barbie now. The way you looked when he married you was pretty all right with him or he wouldn't have married you. Trust me on this—he doesn't somehow expect you to magically appear *more* beautiful than you were when he first met you. It is only if a woman lets herself go that it negatively affects the relationship. Author and speaker Sharon Jaynes has this to say on the subject: "when we decide that we don't care how we look, we are in essence telling our husbands that we don't care about them. . . . Too many of us ladies went to great pains to be attractive to hook the man of our dreams and then, once we reeled him, we let our looks drift out to sea. Unfortunately, when our personal appearance runs amuck on the shores of complacency and laziness, so do our marriages."[1]

Think all men want a woman who looks like a supermodel? Think again. Even though few women believe this, studies show that most men are initially attracted to a woman's eyes and smile, not her body. Additionally, the average guy finds normal-weight women sexier than ultra-thin women.[2] That indicates that you do not have to look like a voluptuous movie star, just that you need to take care of your appearance and look your best for him.

Appearance

Usually the first thing that attracts a man to a woman is her appearance. Many women feel inadequate to live up to that expectation or resent having it placed upon them. Fair enough. But let's look at the other side of the coin. Nearly all women want a man who will be faithful and will provide for them and their children. Those are burdens I don't necessarily always feel adequate to live up to, but I do so because those are the expectations placed upon me as a good husband. It's part of the unspoken agreement I entered into when I got married.

Remember this—*all wives are trophy wives.* Your man wants other men to envy him for the woman who has chosen him. It's a form of validation—it boosts his self-esteem. But even more than that your man needs and wants to figuratively (maybe literally) show you off. That includes your physical appearance as well as all your unique character traits. Women who desire to make their men proud are usually more satisfied with their relationships. A woman who takes care of herself physically and cares about her appearance gives her man a certain status with other men (and quite possibly with other women).

A lot of destruction is being done to women's psyches in this country by the image of female physical perfection that's forced upon them. It is a skewed and distorted version of female design. Hollywood and fashion designers seem determined to insist that women should look more like prepubescent boys. But if you think about the kind of women *men* actually like to look at, I think you will find they are much more full-figured and well-endowed. Previously women like Marilyn Monroe, Jayne Mansfield, and Raquel Welch were popular pinup models. Today more curvaceous women such as Pamela Anderson, Britney Spears, and Jessica Simpson still set the standard. Most men prefer a woman who looks like a woman. A woman who feels good about herself, takes care of herself, and is confident in her femininity can be outside the "fashion design standard" for body size and shape and still be quite attractive to men.

Even if he doesn't consciously realize it, a man will eventually become resentful of his wife if he feels she doesn't care enough about him to try and look attractive for him. This is especially true if he sees her get fixed up to go to work every day, but she doesn't bother to wear makeup or dress nicely when at home or when they go to the store together. Essentially she's saying it's important for her to look nice for others but not him. After all, the women he works with and sees throughout the day are looking their best. Whether you like that or not, it's the way your husband is wired. Over time that resentment will begin to manifest itself by eroding other areas of your relationship. A man's dissatisfaction with his wife's appearance will bleed into other areas of his relationship, causing discontentment and restlessness.

Some women get to a point where they just give up. They figure it's no use, so why try? You try because it matters to him whether you look nice or not. When you don't try it tells him he is not worthy of your effort. It tells him you do not respect him. It tells him you do not love him. In his book *What Makes a Man Feel Loved*, author Bob Barnes says, "When men aren't proud of what they see in their wives, they become more vulnerable to having an affair. . . . Every married woman needs to ask herself, 'Am I looking my best when I am with my husband? Is he proud of my personal appearance?'"[3]

A male reader told me he was embarrassed that his wife had gained a lot of weight since they got married. My first thought was, *Why are you embarrassed? You're not the one who gained the weight.* But he was embarrassed because his wife's weight gain reflected on him as a man and a husband. It told the world she didn't care enough about him to take care of herself and try to keep herself attractive for him. Whether you like it or not, men are judged by the beauty of the women they marry, just like women are judged by the character and status of the men they attract. Men with attractive wives are held in higher regard by both men and women.

Author and psychologist Willard Harley says, "When a man has an attractive wife, it says he has the appeal and talent that deserve someone of her caliber. When a man's wife lets herself become unattractive, the message comes across loud and clear that he couldn't get someone better and probably deserves her. He has little to offer, the world decides, and he attracts little in return."[4]

I'm not saying a woman needs to get fixed up with a full face of makeup every time her husband's around or to get cosmetic surgery to enhance her physical attributes. But it is important for him to see that you think enough of him to still want to be desired by him. Men are extremely visual creatures. It's not so much whether *you* think you are beautiful as the fact that you put some effort into looking nice for him. Knowing you care enough about him to take care of your appearance means a lot to your husband. Just know that men get very frustrated when their wives constantly fret about their physical condition (their weight, for example) but never seem to actually do anything about it.

I actually heard a woman on television admit that the reason she looked so bad was that she had been in a committed relationship for the past seven years and so fashion and looking nice had not been an issue for her. I nearly fell out of my chair. I was shocked to learn that many women unconsciously feel the same way! Trust me, winning a man with your appearance is one of the many tools you have available at your disposal. But that is only the beginning. You have to continue to make that a top priority in your relationship if you don't want to see his desire and your influence wane.

Women who let themselves go or gain a lot of weight after marriage are to some degree violating their marriage vows and the contract they entered into. I'm not talking about temporary setbacks like after childbirth, but a general lack of concern about appearance. It would be similar to a man working very hard before marriage and then never again providing financially for his family after he got the ring on her finger.

There's nothing more flattering and fulfilling to a man than to be wanted physically by a woman. But, all things being equal, is it more gratifying to be wanted by an attractive, well-kept woman or one who's slovenly and out of shape? If I'm being brutally honest, my answer is the first choice. It might not make it right, but that's just the way it is. Men who are not proud of the way their wives look are more vulnerable to having affairs. How a woman takes care of herself speaks directly to the world about how much she loves and respects her husband. And remember, respect is high on the ladder for men.

Keep in mind that men are primarily visual creatures. Thousands of years as hunters made eyesight their sharpest sense. Of course, women already know that. After all, why are the makeup, fashion, dieting, and personal grooming (hair and nail salons, tanning booths, cosmetic surgery, anti-aging treatments, etc.) industries so successful? While men do use these products and services, women are far and away the largest percentage of their clientele.

What's generally the first thing a woman does when she gets divorced or breaks up with her boyfriend? She loses weight, gets herself in shape, buys some new clothes, and starts putting on makeup everywhere she goes. In other words, she makes herself marketable. If she had put that much effort into staying attractive for her husband or boyfriend, would they still be together today? Perhaps that's too harsh. I know that there are any number of reasons people break up or get divorced, and it is seldom a one-way street. My point though is that it is very important to a man that a woman keep herself attractive for him. It doesn't mean that she has to be a ravishing beauty or a skinny little runway model, just that he knows she cares enough about him to make the effort to take care of herself.

Most men I know appreciate everything a wife does to make herself look attractive, whether it's buying new clothes, getting her hair done, or joining a gym. We walk a fine line between encouraging her and being supportive, and getting her mad at us for insinuating she's not attractive. As long as you don't go overboard with the spending, I think most men like it when their wives buy new outfits or go to a salon to get their hair and nails done.

Work on accentuating your positive physical qualities. All women are beautiful in some way or another—it's the gift God gave you when he created femininity. Just as all women have physical characteristics they don't like, you also have some that are very positive—even you have to admit that you like something about your appearance. Determine your positive attributes and then focus on those. Your appearance does not just relate to your physical qualities; it also has to do with fashion, grooming, hair, makeup, style, and even accessories such as shoes and jewelry. Just the way a woman carries herself is often quite appealing—her attitude adds a lot to her appearance. A woman who is comfortable with herself and confident in her femininity is very attractive to men.

I've heard it said that when women are single they dress to impress men, but after they've married they dress for other women. Whether you realize it or not, you *are* dressing for him. I think most men probably feel that the way their woman dresses reflects the way she feels about him.

Your man loves you for who you are, not what you look like. Trust me, he is probably less concerned and critical of your physical imperfections than you are. Don't spend so much time obsessing about your appearance that you become a basket case. After birthing several children, you are not going to look like you did when you were eighteen years old—and your husband doesn't expect you to. Just let him know you care. One way to do that is by making him feel that you want to be attractive for him—he'll appreciate it. And when he complains about why you are taking so long to get ready, just tell him, "I want to make sure I look nice for you." That will shut him up in a hurry.

And even if you sincerely want the truth, for goodness' sakes don't ask him if those shorts make your thighs look fat. He's not going to tell you the truth (not more than once anyway).

Attributes

Here's what most women don't understand—attractiveness, sexiness, and desirability are not just about physical appearance. But because our culture focuses so much on a woman's physical appearance, that is what women obsess about. They worry about trying to live up to some impossible cultural image created by Madison Avenue. For men desirability is more than physical. Physical appearance is certainly important, but not as important as most women think. Women have many, many assets that are attractive to men. God created women to be desired by men—he didn't stipulate that they had to look a certain way before men would be attracted to them. Our culture has perverted that image so that many women do not feel worthy of being desired. Perhaps that's why so many women "settle" for the first man who pays them any kind of attention.

Every woman has some attractive qualities about her merely by virtue of her gender. God has made every woman desirable to some, if not all, men. Most women don't believe that, but I submit that it is true and can in fact be proven. I doubt if there is a woman alive—given she's a normal, healthy woman—who couldn't set out to have sex with a man and have that goal come to fruition within a very short period of time. She might not be able to attract *every* man on the planet, but she could certainly attract *a* man (likely more than one). Most women probably feel that reflects more poorly on the attributes of males than it does on female desirability, but just because a dog will eat whether he is hungry or not does not make the food any less desirable.

A woman's humor, intelligence, vulnerability, and personality can all be attractive and stimulating to a man whether she is classically beautiful or not. We've all seen women who were not what our culture would consider physically attractive who were either married to very handsome, successful men or were surrounded by a bevy of available men.

Attitude and demeanor can be very alluring. Women who enjoy being female and who revel in their femininity are charming to men. A female's grace, softness, and caring are like a cooling breeze on a hot afternoon to a male's rougher demeanor. Her joyful and gentle countenance is a welcome rest from the competitive, rugged world of masculinity.

Women who understand and appreciate their sexuality are enticing to men. Women who enjoy sex are refreshing. The way a woman talks, how she acts, the way she dresses, her hair, clothing, shoes, perfume, and even the jewelry she wears (bracelets, bangles, ankle bracelets, earrings, and toe rings all come to mind) are all capable of stimulating a man's attention.

One man told me he was secretly attracted to a female friend, not because she was sexy or beautiful, but because she had "kissable" lips. Another told me he likes women with well-manicured fingernails and toenails. Still another said the most important attribute to him was how a woman carries herself. When she walks, do her hips gently sway or does she plod along like an East German weightlifter? You don't have to be petite to be graceful—but you do have to care about the image you project.

And finally, even a woman's voice and how she speaks can influence a man's decision-making process (on the West Coast a woman with a Southern accent is always very popular). Women with hoarse or sultry voices have been known to drive men crazy. Actress Sharon Stone made a career out of her voice. Men always fantasize about (and generally overestimate) what female radio DJs look like.

The Six Most Irresistible Inner Qualities for Influencing a Man

A woman's character tells a man what qualities he has to live up to in order to be involved in her life. By emphasizing the importance of certain character traits in her own life, she communicates to a man which character traits she's attracted to and will be satisfied with. By her own focus on developing and maturing in the character traits she's committed to (such as loyalty, integrity, courage, and commitment), she influences those traits in the man she's involved with.

Simply put, if you want a man of character in your life, you need to be a woman of character. Character attracts character. If you compromise on your principles, you will attract (or even create) a man who compromises his principles or worse—a man who has none to begin with.

We men all know we are better people because of the women who marry us. In fact, I've heard it theorized that it is a mother's job to raise her son until she can find a suitable younger woman to finish the task. Every little boy has better table manners when seated with girls. So it is with marriage or relationships. A good woman who partners with a good man makes him even better. The key is that she finds a man with potential and not one who has so many character strikes against him that her powerful influence won't make any difference.

The following are character traits that highly influential women possess in abundance. I looked closely at the handful of women I know who exemplify women of huge influence within their homes. These women all have husbands of exceptional character, ability, and achievement. Were these men that noble before they married? I don't know, but I suspect their wives had a lot to do with them maturing into the men of integrity they are today.

Loyal

When a woman is loyal she brings glory to her husband's name. She supports him publicly and behind the scenes. Her actions are always in the best interests of her husband. Her husband is respected because of the words and actions of his wife. He is truly blessed by her presence next to him. Her husband has confidence in her and trusts her completely because he knows she always has his best interests at heart. She doesn't run off half-cocked and say or do things that require her husband to come along behind her and clean up the mess she created. She lifts him up to others, making sure people are aware of his accomplishments and good deeds.

She dresses in attire that is attractive and classy, appealing but not overtly enticing. She is strong and dignified with firm convictions. Her presence brings glory and pride to her husband's image and reputation. She brings him good, not harm, all the days of her life (Prov. 31:12).

Enterprising

An enterprising woman oversees a well-run household, just as a sea captain runs a tight ship. Whether she works outside the home or not, she watches over the affairs of her household with diligence. She maintains a budget that is within their earnings. Her home is clean and orderly, and each individual contributes their fair share to the operation of the home. She feeds the family well with healthy meals. Her children are never lacking. She is wise and prudent in her shopping habits, having the discipline to wait and obtain good deals. She works diligently and is not a sluggard. Her dealings are never to satisfy self-indulgence or instant gratification. She uses her influence to help her husband understand the dangers of foolish choices and teaches her children to be wise in their spending.

She may even barter goods for something needed in the home. Women in agricultural times were probably more adept at this kind of stewardship than many modern women because the culture forced them to be. Enterprising women might even start a home-based business that successfully contributes to the home. She is well-read and has authority to make decisions on her own. She is multitalented, with money to invest and maybe even real estate to manage. She has the business skills to sell in the marketplace.

Does she save and plan for a rainy day? Can her husband depend on her to be there for him during times of crisis? Is she reliant as part of a team to face the challenges of life? All those attributes make an enterprising woman a highly valued life partner.

Positive/Optimistic

An optimistic woman has a positive attitude, always lifting those around her up and never bringing them down. She exudes feminine grace and beauty. She has a natural elegance that comes from the inside. Her sunny disposition warms those in close proximity. She gives compliments and seldom criticizes without cause. Her tongue, the double-edged sword, is used for soothing and healing and never to strike at the hearts of others.

She knows her neighbors and they rejoice in her presence. She keeps herself healthy and strong. She knows people depend on her.

Men face a lot of rejection in the world—on the job, in relationships, and from nearly every circumstance in life. Because of that they are buoyed by cheerfulness in their women. For instance, I tell women who are interested in getting married to have an optimistic countenance. A woman can be stunningly beautiful, but if she has a sour look on her face most men won't risk approaching her (except conceited jerks). Men are sensitive to whether a woman is encouraging or undermining. If they are going to risk their dignity and self-esteem by approaching her, they want to be reasonably certain she's not going to crush them the minute they step up to the plate.

When your husband comes home from work, does he risk feeling rejected by a wife who acts like a petulant little child, or does he come home to a happy, smiling woman who makes him feel safe and good about being home? If you've ever experienced approaching a sullen teenage girl and being brutally rebuffed, you know how this feels. I once made the mistake of touching my teenage daughter's hair when she was in a snit. It only takes once before you learn not to risk that kind of rejection. Learn to recognize the atmosphere you project.

Caring

A caring woman "opens her arms to the poor and extends her hands to the needy" (Prov. 31:20). She exhibits genuine concern and compassion for those less fortunate, be they humans or animals. Her concern for those who are sick or wounded of heart is an inspiration to those around her. Her compassion translates into actions, making a difference in the world. She treats those around her with respect and dignity. She has a servant's heart.

You can recognize a woman's character by observing how she treats those who serve her, such as waitresses, bus drivers, and grocery checkers. Does she extend courtesy only to those who can be of direct benefit to her, or is she gracious to all who cross her path?

Her children are respectful and call her blessed. Her husband praises her and recognizes her worth and value. Hence he cherishes her and gives honor to her publicly and privately whenever possible. She has calmness and dignity about her. Her countenance and actions provide healing and nurturing in abundance.

Creative

A creative woman finds ways to add to the vitality of her family, be it through new resources or emotional support. She considers obstacles to be challenges and crises to be opportunities. She doesn't pout or become depressed when things do not go as planned. She is persistent in finding new ways to benefit her family. She knows the heart of her husband and each of her children. She finds innovative and invigorating ways to encourage and inspire them. Her efforts are refreshing, like cool water on parched lips.

Righteous

A righteous woman "speaks with wisdom and faithful instruction is on her tongue" (Prov. 31:26). She teaches the young and helps friends with prudent advice. She does not indulge in gossip. Her counsel can be trusted and is sought by young and old alike. Her husband does not have to spend half his time straightening out problems at home. She shows good judgment in all her decisions. She is a virtuous woman; a woman after God's own heart.

This woman prays for her husband daily. She uses her position of influence—as his completer in God's eyes, as his helpmate—to intercede on his behalf. In fact, when she prays for her husband she is actually praying for herself as God has commanded us to "cleave together as one." As you pray for your husband ask for God's blessing over his life. Ask God to give him wisdom and discernment. Petition God to help make him a leader that others look up to. And ask God to help you know how best to use your influence to support and encourage his growth and development.

"Charm is deceptive, and beauty is fleeting; but a woman who fears the LORD is to be praised" (Prov. 31:30). A righteous woman will reap God's blessings and garner praise and eternal rewards for herself and her family. She is a role model for all women, especially her daughters and other young women under her influence.

This is a portrait of ideal womanhood from the Bible. Again, not all men care about every one of these characteristics, but as a rule of thumb I would encourage you to develop as many of them in your life as possible. A woman with these traits is bound to not only make her husband happy, but will likely be more happy and content with her own life.

REAL QUESTIONS FROM REAL WOMEN

Q: **Why do men get so upset about girlfriend time? What do they really think is happening?**

A: I don't know that *all* men get upset about girlfriend time (I encourage it). If they do get upset one reason might be that they are feeling as if they are not getting enough of your time and attention. Another reason is that men know how other men think. Your husband thinks you are as sexy as all get out. Hence he knows other men will be eyeing you and possibly even making passes at you in public. Plus guys know how much trouble they are capable of getting in around their buddies, so they assume it's possible when women get together.

Q: **Why do men freak out when we lose weight?**

A: Surely you jest? Maybe a man who is insecure in his ability to keep his wife might get anxious if she started looking too attractive. Or if a wife struggles with eating disorders or other health issues he might get concerned for her safety. Otherwise, I've never met a man yet who was mad when his wife lost weight. Most of the time women only lose weight when they are getting ready to make a life change— that possibility could be frightening to a man.

eleven

His Cheating Heart

The Grass Is Always Greener

> CNN found that Hillary Clinton is the most admired woman in America. Women admire her because she's strong and successful. Men admire her because she allows her husband to cheat and get away with it.
>
> —*Jay Leno*

As a culture we appear to be sliding down the slippery slope of infidelity with ever greater frequency. As many as 65 percent of men and 55 percent of women will have an extramarital affair by the time they are forty, according to the *Journal of Psychology and Christianity*. Christians are no different than secular men and women in this regard. A *Christianity Today* survey found that 23 percent of the three hundred pastors who responded admitted to sexually inappropriate behavior with someone other than their wives while in the ministry.

While men still commit adultery most frequently, the fastest growing rate of infidelity is among young married women. Many of them have been molested or are the adult children of divorce. They are looking for marriage to make up a deficit that comes from their childhood. "Intimacy deficits" stem from a person's family of origin. They may be from a lack of touching or hugging, from a need for a lot of admiration, affirmation, and adoration, or from another vacuum that a spouse wants satisfied.[1] Unfortunately, even if a spouse knows about these intimacy deficits it is very difficult to fulfill them.

Why do men cheat? Why are they attracted to other women even when they *claim* to love their wives? Why do they look at other women with lust when they have a beautiful, willing wife at home?

Here are some possible insights into why men may be predisposed (or just willing) to lust after women and even stray from their wedding vows. (Before we get started, let me just say that I am in no way condoning this behavior in men. To betray the trust and faith of your spouse and break your wedding vows is unconscionable and despicable behavior. However, many people—men and women—are falling into this trap in increasingly greater numbers. This is a huge problem in a significant number of marriages across the US. This is my attempt to explain possible causes, which will then help you understand how to prevent it from happening.)

Greener Pastures

My wife has been a great wife to me and mother to my children. She has been loyal, supportive, loving, and unselfish toward me for three decades. She frequently (nearly always) puts my needs ahead of her own. She has taken care of me in sickness and in health. She loves and respects me and is a huge encourager. She is a *good* person. She's generally in a good mood and is happy most of the time. She doesn't nag me excessively. She seldom wants or demands material goods. In fact, I usually have to force her to buy clothes or shoes. She's beautiful, sexy, and smart. She's funny, compassionate, a hard worker, and morally upright. I admire and respect her. She is my best friend and has been a great person to spend my life with—better than I deserve. She's a good and decent woman who has always been there when I needed her. I love her more than I have ever loved anyone in my life. In fact, I am more in love with her now than I was when I married her.

And yet, because I'm a man (or else just a pig), I confess I am still physically attracted to other women. I control those urges primarily because of the love and respect I have for my wife. The risk of losing her is not worth the momentary gratification I might receive through a dalliance with another woman. Additionally, I just plain would not want to hurt her that deeply. And yet, I have urges. But even though I have had opportunities over the years to be with other women, how could I betray my wife's loyalty? What would that say about my character as a man if I were to betray her just to satisfy a temporary whim? Author Danielle Crittenden says, "A man stays in marriage not simply because he loves his wife and children, but because he could not respect himself—or expect others to respect him—if he casually up and left, or had an affair, or brought harm to those who so deeply loved and trusted him."[2]

I believe that most if not all men struggle with this issue to some degree or another. Sure, I know men who claim to love their wives so deeply that they are not even slightly attracted to other women (these are usually pastors or other men who have high-profile ministries). I don't disbelieve them, but I suspect that trait is fairly rare.

That being said, as a man I have the capacity of betraying a woman's loyalty, love, and trust without much forethought. We frequently hear about the man who gets caught having a one-night stand and says to his wife, "I love you. It didn't mean anything." This stereotype is likely more true than not. The male ability to compartmentalize areas of our lives enables us to focus on one thing and accomplish great tasks, but it also works against us in that we believe we can isolate specific areas of life without contaminating the rest of it.

As hard as it may be to believe, a man's lust for another woman has nothing to do with how much he does or doesn't love his wife. Being predisposed with the urge to procreate combined with the ability to compartmentalize areas of life so they do not overlap allows men to separate differing segments or areas of their lives. It's why a man can still have sex even if he's been arguing with his wife, whereas a woman needs to resolve the issue before she can physically respond. It's also why a man who knows better is still capable of succumbing to another woman even though he loves his wife.

It also doesn't matter how attractive a man's wife is. We see men married to gorgeous women who still cheat on them. Infidelity is probably more often about getting some emotional need met than it is about fulfilling a physical desire.

And finally, like most men, I'm just vain enough to believe that another woman really *could* be attracted to me, and so I can easily fall for her wiles.

Why Do Men Cheat?

What causes men to betray their marriage vows? First of all, men have sexual images thrust in their faces from the time they wake up in the morning until they go to bed at night. I can't even watch a high school, college, or professional sporting event without having a curvaceous, long-legged cheerleader high kick in front of me or shake her barely contained pom-poms in my face. Television programs show every guy in the cast having sexual advances made toward them by the flawless women they come in contact with each week (that doesn't even count the highly sexualized advertisements and commercials). Movies are worse, where even old guys like me have beautiful young girls attracted to their mature masculinity. Never mind that in real life the physical changes the male body goes through as we age would be guaranteed to repulse a beautiful young woman.

Magazines, billboards, commercials all use sexual images to sell their products. Sex sells and everyone knows it. A partially clothed female body attracts the attention of both male and female buyers. Internet spam pops up every few minutes telling me there are "lonely housewives" or "willing young women" all wanting to have sex with me "right here in my own hometown!" This doesn't even count all the tricks and traps pornographers use to ensnare men whenever possible.

While that's no excuse, this constant, low-grade sexual stimulation overloads and short-circuits our already motivated sexual desire, causing it to falter or, more often, to be hypersensitized, wanting more intensified levels of fulfillment. The desire for more and greater stimulation to gratify this artificially created lust can lead a man to end up in situations where he would never set out to go. An affair is almost never a spontaneous decision but a series of gradual choices that slowly lead to that outcome.

Not only that, but there is a spiritual attack taking place on men. The Evil One knows that knocking off the leadership is the key to taking over. The master of lies waits to attack men who are weak in this area. And so leaders in the church, community, and government suffer more spiritual assault in this and other areas, as do men in general, who are the natural leaders of families. If men betray and abandon their families, the families themselves are more vulnerable to evil's influence and destructive power.

Our thought process can also lead us astray. One thought that frightens (or maybe depresses) many men is the thought that they will never again have sex with a different woman for the rest of their life—which is a very long time. For instance, it is destructive for me to think, *I will never again have sex with another woman (except my wife) for as long as I live.* That thought might be comforting to a woman, but it causes near panic in a man's psyche. If I were to allow myself to dwell on it I could easily talk myself into a bad situation. I have to exercise mental self-discipline to control that thought process. When that biological impulse to procreate kicks in and causes you to fear dying without ever having "mated" with other women, it attacks the core of a male's manhood.

Whether this feeling is true or not, it causes many men to feel that once they lose their sexual power they will be figuratively put out to pasture, fading away into obscurity. It's also why immature men often judge their manhood by the number of women they sleep with.

Additionally, it is destructive to have thoughts that I somehow *deserve* a woman who looks better or takes better care of herself, or is a better housekeeper, or more educated, or more *anything* than my wife. If so, I will begin to feel sorry for myself and justify my actions. As it is, I struggle with looking at other men who are perhaps less accomplished, less educated, or less physically attractive than I perceive myself to be and envy them for having younger, prettier, or somehow classier wives than I do. I might allow myself to think, *Why does he get a woman like that when I don't?* It's not that my wife isn't all those things and more, but it is the false perception that the grass always looks greener on the other side of the fence.

Men cheat for a variety of reasons—none of them good. Some men are weak and lack self-control, while others have psychological problems that compel them to obtain self-esteem or a sense of power from their libido. When men are bored and stuck in a rut they are more likely to stray. Men crave excitement. Additionally, like women, when men do not feel valued, appreciated, or respected they might try and get those needs met in the arms of another. I don't think infidelity for men is ever about love but more often about a sense of excitement, validation, and/or filling a void (like boredom) in their lives. Additionally, when men are under high levels of stress for long periods of time they may view an affair as either a temporary relief from or even a reward for their efforts.

For older men the lust aspect of adultery is at its core more about recapturing youthful excitement than it is about strange sex. Since I've never cheated on my wife, I cannot really speak from experience on this topic. But from the men I have spoken to who have succumbed to this temptation, our perceptions are similar (although I doubt this thought process is a conscious one in most men). Boredom with his life, frustration with his career or other relationships, and the realization that he has not accomplished anything significant in life or is "less than" he anticipated all contribute to a yearning for adventure and excitement.

A man down the street recently left his family and wife of thirty years, bought a Harley-Davidson, and set out to "find" himself. He's had a good job with a utility company since high school, and he led a pretty average middle-class lifestyle. From talking with him and reading between the lines of what he told me, I think I understand why he made the choices he did. He had led a safe, boring life, never taking risks, never doing anything dangerous, adventurous, or thrilling. He played by all the rules and accomplished what our culture says should make you happy and successful. His marriage wasn't bad, just stagnant and predictable. I don't think he is a bad man, but he was bored. As middle age approached he began to realize his mortality. After working the same job for thirty years, same schedule every day, same wife, and same life, a smothering sense of desperation and panic set in. *Is this it? Is this all there is to life?* He began to contemplate how he wanted to live the rest of his life. He decided that he did not want to spend his few remaining years the same way he had spent his entire adult life—in a rut. He was tired of playing by the rules that had not given him any sense of accomplishment or, more importantly, significance. He felt like he was trapped in a suffocating blanket of responsibility. He couldn't breathe. He decided he needed to do something drastically different. As his masculine essence was beginning to fade with middle age, he yearned to feel once again the invigorating essence of life he experienced in his youth. Additionally, he was not a Christian and so did not have a foundational value system to measure these natural desires against. His value system was of the world, which encourages the nobility of seeking one's own happiness and self-gratification. And because societal mores promote that "everyone does it," he convinced himself he somehow deserved to live a life that had more meaning and that was more self-fulfilling.

I have been blessed in the fact that as I approached middle age, God steered me down a life path fraught with danger, risk, and significance. It was filled with fearful challenges that fulfilled my need for adventure and significance. I was constantly blessed to see the fruits of my labor as they impacted and changed the lives of others. Almost daily emails from people whose lives have been blessed through my work have fulfilled my yearning for significance and my innate desire to leave a lasting legacy. This challenging lifestyle in middle age short-circuited my need for adventure and passion that so many men find in the arms of another (often younger) woman.

There's also an element of "familiarity breeding contempt" involved. Frankly, the sex in a long-term relationship can easily become boring. It takes work to make it exciting. After all, after three decades (or even three years) of sex with the same woman things can get repetitious and mechanical—the same sensations, the same sounds, the same smells. Especially if one or both partners are not actively being creative and initiating new adventures (I can hear both of my young adult children—and yours—retching and gagging over the thought of their parents being sexually adventurous), the urge for something new, unique, and exciting can become overwhelming. I suspect most of the erectile dysfunction medication on the market is sold to middle-aged men who have been with the same woman for decades and need a "boost" to overcome the boredom rather than to those with actual physical problems. That in no way diminishes the love a man may feel for a woman; it speaks more to his biological disposition to procreate and the need or desire for new conquests and adventures.

Pornographic Lifestyle

The world has become highly sexualized over the past several decades. Sexually graphic images are commonplace and accepted as part of daily life. Pornography, if not outright embraced by most people, is certainly tolerated without too much resistance from our culture. Money talks. Pornography was a $97 billion industry in 2006 and is growing rapidly every year.[3]

Most married women sincerely believe that their husbands are being unfaithful if they view pornography, and they are deeply hurt by it. One woman friend expressed it this way: "You looking at other women, making comments about other women, or looking at pornography are like cheating on me. It makes me feel like you're comparing me to those models and I will never measure up. This makes me want to hide my body, my heart, and my soul from you. This kills my desire for you and ruins our intimacy."

If men know the above statement is true for their wives and girlfriends, why do they do it? Or as one woman put it, "Why do husbands risk not having the depth of true intimacy with their wives, and truly awesome and ultimate sex with the one they love, just to have some trashy, momentary, empty sex encounter elsewhere?"

In response to that question, I would say that most men probably do not believe they are cheating on their wives by looking at pornography or even by masturbating, and they do not consider either to be a serious offense against their marital vows. I suppose intellectually, at some level, men realize that there is an element of infidelity involved. And obviously Scripture indicates that lusting after anything is sin. But for men, anything short of the physical act of sex is likely to be viewed (at least secretly) as somewhat inconsequential. Of course men, especially men of the church, would not admit that publicly. Granted, they act ashamed, and they go to great lengths to appease their wives and to earn back their trust after being caught (for example, suffering the public humiliation of attending sexual addiction classes)—generally because their wives get so upset and hurt. But I suspect if you surveyed men (even Christian men) anonymously they would not *truly* believe they had committed adultery by indulging in those acts. It doesn't make it any less a sin or any more valid of an excuse, but I truly believe this is how most men look at this issue.

Understand me clearly here—I am not promoting those behaviors as healthy for men. For a lot of reasons they are very unhealthy for men and their relationships. Nor am I condoning or trying to say they are *not* sinful acts. I'm merely pointing out how many men view these situations differently than women might—and I'm not all that convinced that people in the church are much different from those outside the church on this issue. Because I've written extensively about the dangers of pornography to masculinity in my other books I will not repeat myself here. But it is important to recognize the allure and dangers of pornography, especially for men.

More than 70 percent of men ages 18 to 34 visit a pornographic website every month, and approximately 47 percent of Christian families say porn is a problem in their homes. A *Christianity Today* Leadership Survey in 2001 showed that 37 percent of pastors struggle with pornography. A Promise Keepers Survey at a stadium event revealed that 53 percent of the men in attendance admitted to being involved with pornography within one week of the event.[4] Those statistics are somewhat dated and I expect are even worse today.

Therein lies the problem that traps most men into addictions with pornography, which then destroy their relationships and marriages. Pornography *is* so dangerous to men because of their visual nature. Viewing porn releases chemicals that cause a "high" as addicting as cocaine. And like cocaine this addiction needs increasing amounts of more graphic stimulation to re-create the same high. In this way pornography eventually escalates into actual infidelity. Even if it doesn't, it creates unrealistic expectations in men of their wives. Additionally, the selfish process of self-gratification (which is easier than making love to his wife) creates a lack of physical desire for his wife, causing her to feel unloved and worthless.

Porn is so addicting for men that just reading or writing about why it is destructive makes me want to look at it. I have never struggled harder against its pull than when reading a book written for men on how to remain sexually pure. Porn, like most vices and addictions, seems innocent enough at first but gradually leads to the depths of despair.

Her Cheating Heart

Even though love and sex are frequently separate, compart-mentalized issues for men, I couldn't in good conscience step over that boundary. Truthfully, as a man, I am biologi-cally and emotionally *capable* of loving my wife a great deal and would still not be too conflicted about having a physical relationship with another woman. I am capable of compart-mentalizing those areas of my life so that they do not blend into one another.

I don't know if women are wired that way, although I have been told that they are not. Love and sex are much more intertwined as one package within their psyche. Certainly some women are able to overcome that hurdle and have af-fairs with men to whom they are not married. I suspect this is because some basic needs of theirs are not being fulfilled, to the point where they are compelled to try and get them met elsewhere. Frequently though, women engage in long-term affairs of the heart in these circumstances and not one-night stands as men are more apt to do. Or perhaps that is just the way things used to be, and now women are as promiscuous as men.

What with all the talk about men's higher sex drive, I was actually surprised to learn during my research for this book that in approximately 25 percent of marriages the woman actually has a more active libido than the man. For these women, the lower sex drive of their husbands is a source of frustration and even anger (especially when they hear their sisters and girlfriends complain about how their husbands won't quit pestering them). These women feel less attractive to and less desired by their husbands, creating psychological issues such as lower self-image. Since most women derive some amount of self-esteem from being desired by a man, this could cause a woman to seek solace in the desire of another man.

Because God created women with the desire for the security and love of just one man, historically there was less likelihood of affairs happening. Even though men were desirous, women were less willing to participate (it wasn't in their best interests). At least part of the reason for the large increase of extramarital affairs taking place today is not only women's economic independence but also the increase in women viewing pornography. Twenty-eight percent of online porn viewers are women, and that number is growing. This has loosened the social barriers against infidelity and increased the desire women have for illicit sexual activities. The lowering of social mores regarding premarital and extramarital sex, the lack of stigma regarding divorce and single parenting, and the acceptance and cultural promotion of an individual's "right" to self-gratification have encouraged promiscuity in all forms.

Additionally, our culture now teaches girls and young women to be the aggressors in relationships. One of the fallacies that the sexual revolution propagated was that women should be the *same* (not just equal) as men in all ways, especially sexually. Thus women were pushed to act just like men and be sexually aggressive, whether it was healthy for them or not. This has been detrimental to females in several ways, one of which is that it causes males to be lazy, passive, and take women for granted in their relationships. Men get what they want (sex) without having to sacrifice anything in return. Males typically do not appreciate or value things they do not have to work for. So if sex comes too easy, they do not value the vessel.

I'm not saying that a woman's sexual needs are less important or that her sexuality is of lesser value than a man's. I am saying that encouraging women to act like men sexually does not best serve them in the long run. In her book *What Our Mothers Didn't Tell Us*, Danielle Crittenden says, "If men feel that they can flit from woman to woman, they will. They will enjoy our ready availability and exploit it to their advantage. . . . [But] the desire to be pursued and courted, to have sex with someone you love as opposed to just barely know, to be certain of a man's affection and loyalty—these are deep female cravings that did not vanish with the sexual revolution."[5]

Males were created to pursue, women to be pursued. One of the outcomes of hunting for thousands of years is that men like the chase. The chase causes their testosterone levels to rise, which in turn increases sexual desire. This desire to initiate, pursue, and ultimately conquer (figuratively) a woman is part of his biological and psychological makeup. Of course, young men will tell you they like women to make the first move. Well of course they do! It allows them to not have to face their fears, risk potential rejection, or expend any energy. Just like predators in the wild would be ecstatic for their prey to walk up and fall at their feet so they didn't have to expend any energy during the hunt, so also men would prefer women to fall into their beds with no effort or risk on their part. I have had many discussions with younger women who refuse to acknowledge this truth because they have been raised to think that women should be the aggressors and pursue what they want whether it is good for them or not. Many of them find out too late that in the long run this is harmful to their relationships. Frankly, women who approach their sexuality this way are giving away the greatest power they have in life—their sexual power.

Curiously, over the course of thirty years of marriage, my wife has never pointed out a man whom she found attractive. Even though I have been inquisitive and asked her several times over the years, she has never admitted that she thought any movie star or husband of a friend was good looking, sexy, or even handsome. She hasn't even mentioned it in passing. In her wisdom she says that I am the only man for her. Oh, I know she had a crush on Elvis when she was young, but what woman didn't? I'm not stupid enough to think that she doesn't find at least *some* other men attractive (even though I probably do set a pretty high standard), but I believe that her inattention to other handsome males has been healthy for our relationship. Even though I'm pretty secure in my manhood, I'm not sure how well information like that would be received. Would I be jealous if she was physically attracted to another man—even abstractly and from a distance? I don't know—maybe, especially if I allowed myself to dwell upon it. My point is, the fact that she admits to being turned on only by me is somehow honoring in and of itself to my pathetically fragile male ego. Because men are competitive, I know I would be checking (if only unconsciously) to see how I stacked up against the other guy. But I'm still curious about what kind of men she finds attractive.

That's one reason why it is important not to compare your husband with other men—especially in areas where he cannot compete. Saying something like, "You should see the enormous diamond ring Mary's husband just bought her," when your husband is struggling just to pay the bills can send the wrong message. A man who does the best he can in life shouldn't be made to feel less by being compared to a man who has more money, more power, or even more hair than he does.

When a man's spouse cheats on him he feels disrespected. Conversely, when a woman's spouse cheats, to her it seems more about betrayal of trust. I'm sure there are elements of hurt and betrayal for men just like there are feelings of disrespect for women. I have been fortunate to have never personally experienced this type of betrayal in my marriage, but conversations with many men and women confirm this premise. Perhaps because women have a greater need for intimacy to love and engage in sexual activity, the loss of trust is more important to them. And because his wife's respect is core to his self-image, a man is more devastated by its loss than a woman might be. Again, these are generalizations, but anecdotal evidence would appear to bear it out. For instance, many women tell me the lies their husbands told while engaging in an extramarital affair were much more painful and harder to forgive than the actual physical act. As a man I can say without a doubt that the lies would be of secondary importance to the disrespectful physical act of betrayal. It would be an insult to my manhood.

All this to say, both men and women are at risk for infidelity, especially when we are not aware of the factors that motivate us to seek getting our needs met through people other than our spouses.

REAL QUESTIONS FROM REAL WOMEN

Q: **Why do men always feel the need to touch their "junk"?**

A: Just checking to make sure it's still there.

Q: **Why do men have frequent affairs in the work-place?**

A: A man spends more waking hours in the workplace than he does at home. He also interfaces closely with his co-workers in a stressful environment with the objective of meeting goals—something men thrive on. Hence, he spends more face-to-face time with the women he works with than he does his wife. He spends that time in endeavors that tend to create intimacy and bonding in males—goal-oriented pur-suits. If he's not getting his needs met at home, his fe-male co-workers start looking like good alternatives.

twelve

His Needs of His Woman

> I should like to see any kind of a man, distinguishable from
> a gorilla, that some good and even pretty woman could not
> shape a husband out of.
>
> —*Oliver Wendell Holmes*

One of the men I admire most is John Wooden, the legendary coach of the UCLA Bruins college basketball team. Coach set a number of records that will probably never be broken, including winning ten NCAA championships over a twelve-year period (seven in a row) and winning eighty-eight straight games during one stretch. Beloved and revered by his players, he changed the lives of every young man who played for him through the powerful values and life lessons he taught them.

But of perhaps more importance, Coach Wooden was married for fifty-three years to the love of his life, Nell. Coach

Wooden was so dedicated to her that after her death in 1985, he continued to write Nell a love letter every month for the next twenty-five years. He faithfully placed those letters under her pillow on her side of the bed until he finally passed away in 2010, going to be with his beloved wife.

I don't know what kind of woman inspires that kind of love in a man, but I do know this is the kind of man I want to learn about relationships from. Coach Wooden had this to say about marriage:

> Love means many things. It means giving. It means sharing. It means forgiving. It means understanding. It means being patient. It means learning. And you must always consider the other side, the other person. You can give without loving, but you cannot love without giving. . . . Young couples get married and don't realize it's different from courtship. You have to work at your marriage; it's two-sided, and you'd better realize that.[1]

I think Coach was trying to say that we need to be willing to eagerly fulfill the needs of our spouse if we want to have a successful marriage. Here are some needs that men need fulfilled by a good wife.

The Need for Companionship

One of a man's greatest needs is companionship. God knew that when he said, "It is not good for the man to be alone. I will make a helper suitable for him" (Gen. 2:18). The New King James version renders this passage, "I will make him a helper comparable to him." God then went on to create all the animals of the world and paraded them in front of Adam one by one for him to name. I think God did this so that when Adam met Eve he would recognize that she was not just another creature but something very special. God knew that without female companionship and a partner for reproduction, the man could never fully realize his humanity.

When a lonely Adam saw Eve for the first time, he said (in shock and awe, I imagine), "This is now bone of my bones and flesh of my flesh; she shall be called 'woman' for she was taken out of man" (Gen. 2:23). The phrase "This is now" means "At last!" Adam immediately recognized that Eve was a *part* of him. It must have been exhilarating for Adam—like looking in a mirror at an image of himself, yet at something wonderfully different and unique. She was a perfect match for him. She was formed from bone and not from clay like the other animals. She was created as an equal to be a companion and a completer so that Adam was whole. She was the completion of what God started with Adam. She made him whole—like two halves coming together as one. She was his sustainer, not his servant. The fact that Adam named her *woman*—a derivative of *man*—shows that he clearly understood Eve was equal in every way and perfectly suited for him.

Some Bible interpreters have insisted that "helpmate" means that a woman should be subservient. But helper or helpmate is not meant to be demeaning, as it is the same word God uses regarding himself when he comes to our aid. In fact, the original wording of the verse is "help meet," which means "fitting helper." Thus the verse could be translated that God intended to create a helper that was a perfect fit for man— equal and appropriate in every way. John Eldredge points out that this word (*ezer kenegdo*) is notoriously difficult to translate and is far more powerful than just "helper" but actually means "lifesaver."[2] Helper or helpmate might also be translated as "rescuer." Sharon Jaynes says, "What exactly did Eve 'rescue' Adam from? Perhaps it was loneliness. For God had said, 'It is not good for man to be alone.'"[3]

Quite frequently during the dating process a woman accompanies a man on all the things he likes to do. That is one of the things that draws him closer and creates intimacy with her. Many times after they get married she stops hanging out with him and doing things he enjoys. While a man does need time with other men, I think most women would be surprised at how much a man desires his wife to be by his side. Your husband wants to *do* things with you. He wants you by his side during recreational activities.

I always miss my wife whenever I am traveling. Every time I do something new, meet interesting people, or see something incredible, I wish she were there to share it with. This is the intimacy of doing things together—it's how males bond. You'll notice when males get together they are generally doing some activity. They go to the game, they go fishing or hunting, they play cards, they go to the hot rod show. They seldom just sit and chat.

Your husband likes your companionship, even if you don't do the same things. I played basketball for many years in a men's league. Even though I wasn't a star player, I always wanted my wife at the games to cheer for me and be on hand in case I accidently made a fantastic play—which did happen occasionally (well, seldom actually). Especially in those later years when I was so much older than everyone else, whenever I did make a good play everyone took notice. Having her there to witness that inspired me in ways hard to describe. We men all want to be heroes or stars in front of our wives.

My wife attended a knife and gun show with me last summer. I go every year but this was the first time she ever went with me. While she was probably bored wandering through that huge exhibition center (although I think she was a bit interested in all the strange people and bizarre weapons on display), we still had a great time together and I was glad to share her company.

That's not to say that it's not important for you and your husband to have separate interests and time apart from each other. I don't have any desire to attend the big bridal shows she likes going to, and I don't expect her to go deer or elk hunting with me (although I'd love it if she did). But you can still enter into each other's hobbies even if you don't normally participate. One year my wife went wilderness camping with me. She doesn't particularly like sleeping in the dirt or eating freeze-dried food, but she does know how much I love her companionship in the things I enjoy doing.

The Need for Forgiveness

> Once a woman has forgiven her man, she must not reheat his sins for breakfast.
>
> —*Marlene Dietrich*

Forgiveness is a powerful gift that a woman can give her husband. Forgiveness is an area some women struggle with. Women seem to have much longer memories than men, especially in the area of men's mistakes. My wife can recall at will nearly everything I've ever said or done to hurt her by date, time, and severity of incident for the past thirty years. Once I get something off my chest, most of the time I forget about it and move on. But my wife is a bit strong-willed and has been known to be a tad hardheaded from time to time. Once she gets something stuck in her craw she gnaws on it and growls at it like a little terrier until she gets her point across. Sometimes I just want to throw my hands in the air and say, "Okay, you win! Can we please just drop it now?" Her willingness to generously forgive my mistakes allows me to learn and grow from them. If my wife were to harbor ill will toward me for extended periods of time it would cast a pall over our relationship.

One way a woman can be proactive about offering forgiveness is to *work on her husband's strengths not his weaknesses*. This is counter to what most segments of our society tell us, which is that we need to work on our weaknesses not our strengths (especially husbands). But that is a form of criticism, not encouragement. Most men are already well aware of their shortcomings. Nurturing your husband's areas of strength is encouraging and uplifting. Women of influence and forgiveness nurture strengths instead of exploiting weaknesses.

Don't just focus on the things your man does wrong. Study him carefully to find out what his strengths and weaknesses are. Try focusing on the things he does right rather than being overly critical of his weaknesses. Then help him understand his strengths—his gifts from God. Many people do not know what their strengths or weaknesses are. All of us have been blessed with certain skills and find ourselves lacking in others. Find out where he excels and help him cultivate those strengths to succeed in life. Encourage him to develop those gifts. When we use our God-given gifts to their potential we lead very fulfilling lives.

Be intentional about understanding what strengths you have that he doesn't, and what strengths he has where you are weak. Embrace your differences. Then use your strengths, without making a big deal out of it, to help him succeed. That's not manipulating him; it's partnering with him to use your strengths to compensate for the areas where he is lacking. God gave you this incredible influence in your man's life to empower him. Power is given by God to serve others, not to enslave or crush them.

Couples who are able to recognize each partner's strengths and weaknesses and then most effectively work together as a team are the ones who are the happiest and most satisfied in their relationships. In addition, understanding the areas where your husband is weak allows you to have compassion and forgive him more easily.

The Need for Encouragement and Appreciation

All men want to be appreciated. And I think most men do not feel appreciated for the sacrifices they make, although I doubt that very few men express that feeling. Being appreciated is one of a man's primary needs. He measures himself through his achievements and needs them to be recognized. When a woman seeks appreciation she is likely seeking to be understood and validated. Men derive their worth from what they *do*, while women derive their worth more from who they *are*.[4]

My wife shows me she loves and appreciates me in a variety of little ways. She screens telephone calls for me so I'm not bothered by telemarketers or other people who would want to waste my time. She protects me from people who would like to monopolize my time at events or who want to do me emotional damage. She brings me a glass of ice water when I mow the lawn. She goes out of her way to buy my favorite foods. And at dinner she always serves me first before anyone else. These are small things maybe, but they show me she genuinely appreciates me.

But she also shows me she loves and appreciates me in big ways. I have chronic lower back pain due to degenerative arthritis in my spine (too many years pounding up and down the basketball court). Standing and speaking for long periods of time aggravates my condition. My wife massages my back after each speaking engagement, offering me some level of relief. I consider it a big sacrifice on her part to do this, and her appreciation greatly encourages me to continue through difficult circumstances. To me it shows how much she loves me.

The Need to Dream[5]

Being an average guy with a job, a wife, a mortgage, and 2.5 children can be a little boring. It often seems like all work and no play. All boys and young men grow up with dreams of glory and honor. They envision themselves as stars of the World Series or heroes on the battlefield. They picture themselves overcoming impossible odds—wounded and exhausted—to eventually and oh-so-gallantly win an epic battle between good and evil. Watch little boys at play as their imaginations run wild with the possibilities of life. Most of us never dreamed we would get old and end up as an accountant, a bank loan officer, or a hardware store owner. Since for many men what they do for a living defines who they are, they often end up dissatisfied or frustrated with their lot in life. This has been the case for many years. In 1854, Henry David Thoreau alluded to this with his famous quote, "The mass of men lead lives of quiet desperation."

It's not that men don't enjoy and get fulfillment from their wives and children. It's just that most yearn for lives of significance—to be remembered for something other than how many cars they sold or loans they closed. The burdens and stresses of providing food, shelter, and the day-to-day necessities for a family can be daunting. The challenge becomes to find something that brings significance in what he does, some goal or vision to work toward that inspires and inflames his passion.

Having a woman who encourages his dreams can fulfill a man's need for risk and adventure that all men possess, even if it's buried deep within his soul. But a woman who laughs at a man's dreams, calling them foolish or childish, causes him to stuff his need for release even deeper. Some men eventually become so desperate to release this need for "something they can't quite put their finger on but they know that this just can't be all that life is about" that they start making foolish choices and ruin their lives and the lives of those around them.

Ask your husband about his dreams. Encourage him to discover something he is passionate about. Ask him, "If time and money were no object, what would you want to spend the rest of your life doing?" Even if he never acts on his dreams, it is important for a man to have them.

Men crave adventure. Most men who have affairs do so not because of lust but for the adventure. Your husband needs something positive that he can be passionate about. He needs to feel like he is doing something worthwhile to leave his mark in life. He needs an adventure and a purpose. He needs to know his life means something—that it is significant. Help your husband find an adventure that he can be passionate about. Then be supportive of that dream.

Our ministry, Better Dads, is an awesome adventure in helping to change the world for the better. We reach out to a hurting world with love and grace by easing the burdens of others with hope and encouragement. We believe that we can change the world by helping one man, one woman, one child at a time. This means presenting fathering workshops to inspire and equip men to be more involved in the lives of their children. It means giving seminars for mothers to help them raise boys to become men of character. It means offering classes for prison inmates on authentic masculinity and fathering. It means developing mentoring programs for fatherless boys. It means having weekend retreats for women on choosing healthy relationships. It means teaching workshops for couples on how to have a successful marriage. And these are only the programs God has placed in our hands to date. God continues to grow us and our ministry nearly every day in miraculous ways.

My wife, Suzanne, was instrumental in the development of this ministry. Because of her support I am now living the satisfying and fulfilling life I've always dreamed of and secretly yearned for—a life of significance and adventure. She encouraged me when I did not think I had anything to offer the world. She believed in me when I didn't believe in myself. After God placed his vision on my heart, she supported and encouraged me in every way. Anytime there was a decision that required spending money to do something that would further my growth and help the ministry, she insisted I do it regardless of the cost to us or the inconvenience to her.

Even when the decision was made to close my business of sixteen years and step out in faith on God's provision to go full time in this ministry, she was more excited than I was at the prospect of losing our financial security. For a wife to make that kind of sacrifice requires a remarkable woman with a great amount of trust in God, and from my perspective, a great deal of confidence in me. I do my best to make sure I don't let her down.

We need to look at marriage as a long-distance race, not a sprint. Look at the big picture from a long-term perspective. Even if he never does anything with them, a man needs to dream about things greater than he is. So listen to your husband's dreams. Encourage those dreams, even if you think they are unreachable. He will love and appreciate the fact that you encouraged him rather than discouraged him. Later in life, he will look at you and say, "Honey, you were *with* me," not "If only . . ."[6]

The Need to Feel Cared For

Another great need every man has is to be cared for by a woman who loves him. Life takes its toll on men, and they yearn for someone to care for and nurture them.

I hear women saying all the time about their husbands, "He's such a baby when he gets sick," "I feel like I have another child," or "He acts like I'm his mother." Sounds familiar, doesn't it?

A man needs a loving wife to take care of him. He needs the emotional nurturing only she can give him. Yes, men do often act like babies when they are sick or injured (there's a logical rationale why God chose women to give birth and not men). But there are good reasons for this. Most men have been raised by a mother who nurtured them and took care of their needs. Generally, most men were not raised to be the caretakers within a family. They grow to expect this kind of loving care from women who love them. Husbands generally learn to nurture others by the example modeled for them by their wives. For instance, I probably wouldn't have thought twice about anyone else's needs when I was a young man, but my wife's nurturing of me made me *want* to respond in kind to her.

I'm not sure most men consciously recognize this need for emotional nurturing, but in their hearts they know they need what a woman brings to the relationship. It is one of the reasons men can be such babies when we are sick—we desire that nurturing touch from a woman. And when the world is beating us up we need the restorative healing that a woman's touch brings. Her understanding and empathy is important in grounding us when the world crashes down upon us. A woman's belief in a man empowers him like nothing else. His need for her respect and admiration is foundational in his self-esteem and belief in himself.

The Need for Downtime

One of the things a man needs in order to live a healthy, happy life is time alone to think and process information and emotions. This also allows him to recharge his batteries before becoming engaged in life again.

A man needs time to himself. Often when he comes home from work it takes a while for him to disengage from work mode and transfer into family mode. Having time to himself helps him facilitate this change. Males process information and emotions by thinking about them instead of talking about them like females often do. Additionally, when a man has been under a lot of stress and pressure he may need to get away by himself to feel grounded and get his bearings back.

I frequently speak in front of large crowds. Afterward many people usually want my attention. My wife thrives in that environment. While I function well in that environment for short periods of time, I always need to get away by myself in order to recharge and decompress. The noise and closeness to people eventually wears me down. If I am forced to continually be "on" I start shutting down. If that continues I may even become rude (or at least people may perceive my actions that way). My wife knows this and helps me take a short break in our hotel room or some other quiet venue where I can be alone and regroup.

The truth is most men get beat up in a variety of ways through their jobs and life in general. Maybe your husband has a boss who berates him or is unappreciative of his efforts, or perhaps his job is physically straining or emotionally draining. Perhaps he's under constant financial pressure, is in a tumultuous relationship with someone he loves, or has a child with an illness.

Regardless of the circumstances, men need downtime to recharge their batteries. This is not so much *physical* downtime as it is *emotional* and *psychological* downtime. He needs to regroup and ready himself for the next day or week's challenges.

Also, don't volunteer your husband's time and energy without consulting him first. Most men need downtime in order to reenergize themselves. Downtime is accomplished through hobbies, simple chores, or even watching television (I am as quick and deadly with the television remote as an old west gunfighter). If you keep your man hopping with helping your friends and neighbors, he'll never have time to get rejuvenated.

That is why having an opportunity to relax is so important to a man's health and well-being. Even men who are driven or have type A personalities occasionally need time to sit in front of the television and watch mindless sitcoms or sports programs. Many men look forward to the weekend as a time to watch a few ball games and reinvigorate themselves for the coming week when they will be required to expend all their mental, emotional, and psychological energy all over again. Many of them don't like or are disgruntled with their jobs. Oftentimes their jobs are not challenging or stimulating and give no sense of satisfaction. Frequently a man does not feel he is living a life of significance through the work he does. This exacerbates the problem, paralyzing him into inaction and sometimes depression.

The Need to Be Needed

Not to be needed is slow death for a man.

—*John Gray*

I need to be needed by my wife and children. I love it when my wife needs me for something, even if it's just opening a jar of pickles. I even (if somewhat blusteringly and begrudgingly) relish the fact that the dog and cat need me to feed and water them. I like it when my kids need something from me. I love to provide and protect those under my charge. I feel alive and necessary when I am needed. I like to rescue those I care about whenever I can. Don't think for a minute that if I get a phone call in the middle of the night from a stranded kid I won't immediately spring into action like some tattered, middle-aged superhero. I like it when my adult children call me and ask for advice—they still need the old man. Look at how men naturally, even eagerly, rush to respond in the event of natural disasters or emergency situations.

Clinical psychologist Toni Grant offers this advice to women: "It is important that a man feels that he fulfills a purpose in your life, that he somehow makes the woman feel better, safer, and more beautiful than she was before. He needs to know that his masculine presence makes a difference to her feminine well-being; otherwise two people may have met person to person, but not man to woman."[7]

When my wife needs me it allows me to fulfill my God-created role as provider and protector. When she asks me for help I am excited to lend a hand. If no one needs me, what good am I—what value is my life? Without those roles my purpose in life is taken away.

Women today are much more self-sufficient and self-reliant than they were in the past. Most women today are capable of earning enough income to support themselves and even their families. Many believe they can raise their children on their own and even live a life without a man. In fact, men aren't even necessary to produce children anymore. As civilization has developed a system with police, judges, jails, and an armed militia, men are no longer needed to protect the average woman on a day-to-day basis. Hence, most of the reasons for men being needed (and valued) have been eradicated from our culture. Without those traditional roles many men are floundering, seeking a purpose in life. What is their reason for existence without some purpose that defines them?

Our goal then is to help men define why they are necessary—why they are needed. Yes, women can create and even raise children without the presence of a man, but those children's lives are enriched by a good male role model. Males' creativity and their powerful ability to build things remain vital today. Yes, we have police officers, judges, and laws to protect women and children, but they are still preyed upon without the presence of a good man in their lives. Every measurable category of well-being is negatively impacted in the lives of women and children when responsible masculinity is absent—just look at the lives of families in urban areas with up to an 80 percent fatherless rate where there are virtually no men present.

Men who retire often feel they are not needed around the home or at work anymore. Those men tend to fade from life rather quickly. But when a man is needed he thrives. My dad is quite the handyman. His wife, Dottie, is always asking him to come to her social club and help fix something or move something for them. As all the elderly ladies ooh and aah over his ability to fix things and his overall manliness, he stands quite a bit taller than his older male friends.

So men *are* needed. As a wife, make sure your husband knows that he is necessary and that your life is enhanced through your need for him. Your need is a blessing in his life that gives it substance and meaning.

Getting Your Needs Met

My wife frequently tells women that they will never get their needs met until they meet their husband's needs first. It is her opinion that males are incapable of fulfilling other people's needs until theirs are met. She believes that women have been uniquely qualified by God to fulfill that role. She tells women they have to *temporarily* set aside their needs and meet the needs of their husbands first. Then they can get their needs met. She says women are capable of doing this—they do it all the time with their children. Perhaps that's true.

Men seem to be preoccupied with or unable to focus on anything else when they have an unfulfilled need. (Ever tried to talk to a man when he's hungry—or in the mood for sex?) Perhaps old survival instincts steer a man to focus on himself before being able to focus on others. Again, this makes sense in light of a man's historic role as the sole protector and provider for his clan. A man's death or illness virtually guaranteed the death of his family. Therefore, it was only logical that a man's needs were met first so that he could then fulfill the needs of others. In nature, it's why even though the female lions do the hunting, the mighty male gets to eat first. It's so he's prepared to protect and defend the pride if needed.

I've been really careful over the years never to dispel my wife's theory. Not only do I think it shows incredible wisdom on her part, but who am I to not take advantage of a situation when it presents itself.

REAL QUESTIONS FROM REAL WOMEN

Q: **What is the perfect wife in a man's eyes?**

A: Does the term "Stepford" mean anything to you? Just kidding. I don't think there is a perfect wife—at least not "one size fits all." I do think, in general, that men have lower expectations of their wives than women do of their husbands. I think a man whose wife respects him, cares for him, and generally enhances (completes) his life as an equal partner would be considered a terrific blessing.

Conclusion

And so ends our journey into the soul of a man. Hopefully you have gleaned some insights on what a man needs, his expectations, and what he desires from a wife and a woman. It is my hope that you use that knowledge to become the woman of your husband's dreams—a woman he cherishes above all else. Most of all, please remember to include God in your marriage. The three strands of husband, wife, and God are unbreakable.

Many times throughout the course of your marriage you will need to look to your heavenly Father to fulfill some need, answer a powerful request, or address a debilitating hardship. When you bring God your wounds, needs, and those frustrating issues that are inevitable in a relationship, he is faithful to answer with the response that is best for your life.

Your husband cannot meet all your needs—he's just a man. But God can—he's willing and able to provide the unconditional love and forgiveness that you need in order to be the kind of woman any man would thank God for having in his life. Bon voyage!

Acknowledgments

Thanks to all the people at my publisher who allow me the privilege of living a life of significance. As my son says, "Dad, you've got the best job in the world! People actually *pay* you to tell them your opinion!" Ahem . . . yes, well. Thanks to my awesome editor, Vicki Crumpton, for allowing me to push the envelope, even when it makes her uncomfortable (and also for keeping me from offending vast quantities of people). Thanks to Michele Misiak for your unflagging support and encouragement, and for allowing me to rant and rave every so often without judging me. Thanks to Barb Barnes and the other in-house editors who make my books so much better than they were originally—I appreciate all you do even if I snipe and pout at your suggestions from time to time. Thanks also to the sales staff at Revell and Baker—the unsung heroes of publishing. Thanks for all you do to get my books into the hands of people who need hope and encouragement in their lives. I never get to see you in person to tell you, but please know I appreciate all your efforts.

Thanks most of all to my readers—especially those who fill out my surveys and take the time to share their life experiences with me. Without your willingness (and courage) to be open and vulnerable, multitudes of people's lives would not be touched (and in some small way healed) by your stories. May God bless your faithfulness and generous spirits.

Notes

Chapter 1 What's with His Mother Anyway?

1. Patricia McBroom, "Of Men and Their Mothers: Challenging Freud's Theory," *Berkeleyan* (campus newspaper), January 28, 1998, http://berkeley.edu/news/berkeleyan/1998/0128/menandmothers.html.

2. Paul Coughlin, *Unleashing Courageous Faith* (Minneapolis: Bethany House, 2009), 20.

Chapter 2 His Father

1. Pat Williams with Jim Denney, *Coach Wooden: The Seven Principles That Shaped His Life and Will Change Yours* (Grand Rapids: Revell, 2011), 26.

2. Michael Gurian, *A Fine Young Man* (New York: Putnam, 1998), 72.

3. John Sowers, *Fatherless Generation* (Grand Rapids: Zondervan, 2010), 30.

4. Center for Disease Control (CDC), "Attention-Deficit/Hyperactivity Disorder, Data & Statistics in the US," accessed November 10, 2010, http://www.cdc.gov/ncbddd/adhd/data.html.

5. Sowers, *Fatherless Generation*, 37.

6. Sowers, *Fatherless Generation*, 41, as cited in Megan Bear, "Early Parental Loss a Risk Factor for Adult Psychiatric Illness," http://meganbear.org/fatherlessstats.htm.

Chapter 3 His Relationships

1. Excerpted from J. S. Salt, *How to Be the Almost Perfect Wife* (Thousand Oaks, CA: Shake It Books, 2000).

2. Bill Farrel, *The 10 Best Decisions a Man Can Make* (Eugene, OR: Harvest House, 2010), 121.

3. Kata Fustos, "Marriage Benefits Men's Health," Population Reference Bureau, September 2010, http://www.prb.org/Articles/2010/us marriagemenshealth.aspx.

4. Richard Niolon, review of *The Case for Marriage: Why Married People Are Happier, Healthier, and Better Off Financially*, by Linda J. Waite and Maggie Gallagher, *PsychePage*, October 23, 2010.

Chapter 4 His Communication

1. Joseph Finder, *Power Play* (New York: St. Martin's Press, 2007), 50.

2. Farrel, *The 10 Best Decisions a Man Can Make*, 122.

3. Stephen Hunter, *Pale Horse Coming* (New York: Simon & Schuster, 2001), 109.

4. Scott Haltzman, M.D., and Theresa Foy DiGeronimo, *The Secrets of Happily Married Women* (San Francisco: Jossey-Bass, 2008), 67.

5. *Wikipedia*, s.v. "Physical Law," last modified February 10, 2012, http://en.wikipedia.org/wiki/Physical_law.

6. Frank Pittman, *Man Enough* (New York: Putnam, 1993), 16.

7. John T. Molloy, *Why Men Marry Some Women and Not Others* (New York: Warner Books, 2003), 124.

8. Gary and Barbara Rosberg, *Divorce-Proof Your Marriage* (Wheaton: Tyndale, 2002), 212.

Chapter 5 His Work

1. Adapted from Rick Johnson, *The Man Whisperer* (Grand Rapids: Revell, 2008), and Rick Johnson, *That's My Teenage Son* (Grand Rapids: Revell, 2011).

2. Adapted from Rick Johnson, *The Power of a Man* (Grand Rapids: Revell, 2009).

3. Rick Johnson, *Becoming Your Spouse's Better Half* (Grand Rapids: Revell, 2010).

4. Excerpted from Johnson, *Becoming Your Spouse's Better Half*.

Chapter 6 His Sexuality

1. Sharon Jaynes, *Becoming the Woman of His Dreams* (Eugene, OR: Harvest House, 2005), 240.

2. Quoted in John Eldredge, *Wild at Heart* (Nashville: Thomas Nelson, 2001), 37.

3. Margaret F. Brinig and Douglas W. Allen, "These Boots Are Made for Walking: Why Most Divorce Filers Are Women," *American Law and Economics Review* (2000), 128.

4. Today Health, "Half of Men Would Dump Woman Who Got Fat," poll conducted by AskMen and Cosmopolitan.com, July 26, 2011, http://today.msnbc.msn.com/id/43898300.

Chapter 7 His Need for Respect and Admiration

1. Robert Lewis and William Hendricks, *Rocking the Roles: Building a Win-Win Marriage* (Colorado Springs: Navpress, 1991), 120.

2. Salt, *How to Be the Almost Perfect Wife*, 24.

3. Quoted in Bob Barnes, *What Makes a Man Feel Loved* (Eugene, OR: Harvest House, 1998), 183.

4. Willard Harley, *His Needs, Her Needs* (Grand Rapids: Revell, 1986), 159.

5. *The Nelson Study Bible, New King James Version* (Nashville: Thomas Nelson, 1997), 11.

6. Jaynes, *Becoming the Woman of His Dreams*, 51.

Chapter 8 His Odds of Meeting Your Expectations

1. The 1994 trial of a 24-year-old manicurist from Venezuela cutting off her husband's penis to avenge what she said was years of abuse and rape.

2. Danielle Crittenden, *What Our Mothers Didn't Tell Us* (New York: Simon & Schuster, 1999), 93.

3. Eldredge, *Wild at Heart*, 189–90.

4. Farrel, *The 10 Best Decisions a Man Can Make*, 121.

5. Ibid.

6. Brinig and Allen, "These Boots Are Made for Walking," 126–69.

7. Salt, *How to Be the Almost Perfect Wife*, 28.

8. Today Health, "Half of Men Would Dump Woman Who Got Fat."

Chapter 9 His Emotions

1. University of Pennsylvania School of Medicine, "Brain Imaging Shows How Men and Women Cope Differently Under Stress" (November

19, 2007), *ScienceDaily*, http://www.sciencedaily.com/releases/2007
/11/071119170133.htm.

2. Michael Gurian, *The Wonder of Girls* (New York: Atria Books, 2002), 34.

3. Gurian, *A Fine Young Man*, 38–39.

4. Ibid., 38–40.

5. Michael Gurian, *The Wonder of Boys* (New York: Putnam, 1998), 19.

6. Haltzman and DiGeronimo, *The Secrets of Happily Married Women*, 27.

7. The information from here to the end of the chapter was gleaned from chapter 6 of Johnson, *That's My Teenage Son*.

8. Haltzman and DiGeronimo, *The Secrets of Happily Married Women*, 67.

Chapter 10 His Desires in a Wife

1. Jaynes, *Becoming the Woman of His Dreams*, 62.

2. Ibid., 63.

3. Barnes, *What Makes a Man Feel Loved*, 86–87.

4. Quoted in Jaynes, *Becoming the Woman of His Dreams*, 66.

Chapter 11 His Cheating Heart

1. Cindy Crosby, "Why Affairs Happen," *Kyria*.com, http://www.kyria.com/topics/marriagefamily/marriage/helphealing/3.30.html.

2. Crittenden, *What Our Mothers Didn't Tell Us*, 104.

3. Jerry Ropelato, "Internet Pornography Statistics," *Top 10 Reviews*, http://internet-filter-review.toptenreviews.com/internet-pornography-statistics.html.

4. TechMission, Safe Families, "Statistics on Pornography, Sexual Addiction and Online Perpetrators," http://www.safefamilies.org/sfStats.php.

5. Crittenden, *What Our Mothers Didn't Tell Us*, 35, 39.

Chapter 12 His Needs of His Woman

1. Coach John Wooden with Steve Jamison, *Wooden: A Lifetime of Observations and Reflections on and off the Court* (Contemporary Books: Chicago, 1997), 18.

2. Eldredge, *Wild at Heart*, 51.

3. Jaynes, *Becoming the Woman of His Dreams*, 130.

4. Les Parrott III and Leslie Parrott, *Saving Your Marriage Before It Starts* (Grand Rapids: Zondervan, 1995), 105.

5. Excerpted from Johnson, *The Man Whisperer*, chap. 10.

6. Salt, *How to Be the Almost Perfect Wife*, 16.

7. Toni Grant, *Being a Woman* (New York: Random House, 1998), 68–69.

Bestselling author and speaker **Rick Johnson** founded Better Dads, a fathering skills program based on the urgent need to empower men to lead and serve in their families and communities. Rick's books have expanded his ministry to include influencing the whole family, with life-changing insights for men and women on parenting, marriage, and personal growth. He is a sought-after speaker at many large conferences across the United States and Canada and is a popular keynote speaker at men's and women's retreats and conferences on parenting and marriage. Rick is also a nationally recognized expert in several areas, including the effects of fatherlessness, and has been asked to teach at various educational venues.

To find out more about Rick Johnson, his books, and the Better Dads ministry, or to schedule workshops, seminars, or speaking engagements, please visit www.betterdads.net.

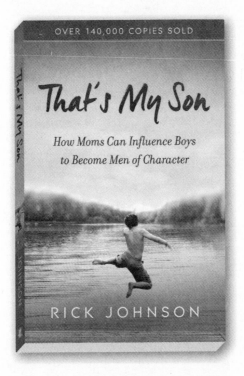

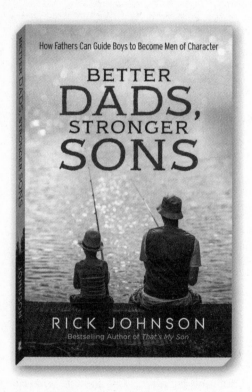

You Can Be a Good Parent
Even If You Didn't Have a Great Example

With Rick as your sympathetic guide, you can break the cycle of abuse, neglect, or absenteeism and create a positive family environment now and for the future.

Meet

RICK JOHNSON
at www.BetterDads.net

Connect with Rick on Social Media

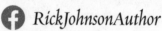 *RickJohnsonAuthor*

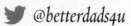 *@betterdads4u*